CO-DEPENDENCY

A book of readings reprinted from *FOCUS on Family and Chemical Dependency,* compiled and published by The U.S. Journal of Drug & Alcohol Dependency and Health Communications, Inc.

Health Communications, Inc.
Deerfield Beach, Florida

Published by: Health Communications, Inc.
3201 S.W. 15th Street
Deerfield Beach, Florida 33442

ISBN 0-932194-21-4

Printed in the United States of America

_____AUTHOR CREDITS_____

Sharon Wegscheider-Cruse, M.S.W.
President, ONSITE
Rapid City, SD
Author of *Choicemaking*

Gerald Shulman
Vice President, Clinical Programs
Addiction Recovery Corporation
Waltham, MA

John Friel, Ph.D.
Director, Counseling Associates
St. Paul, MN
Author of *Adult Children: Dysfunctional Families*

Kathy Capell-Sowder
Family Counselor
Greene Hall Outpatient Services
Dayton, OH

Robert Subby, M.A.
Executive Director, Family Systems Center
Minneapolis, MN
Author of *Lost In The Shuffle*

Terence T. Gorski, M.A., C.A.C.
President, Alcoholism Systems Associates
Hazel Crest, IL

Jael Greenleaf
President, Greenleaf & Associates
Director, The 361 Foundation
Los Angeles, CA

John Wallace, Ph.D.
Director of Treatment, Edgehill Newport
Newport, RI

Charles L. Whitfield, M.D.
Associate Professor of Family Medicine
University of Maryland School of Medicine
Baltimore, MD
Author of *Healing The Child Within*

Marilyn Mason, Ph.D.
Family Therapist/Trainer
Family Therapy Institute
St. Paul, MN

Merlene Miller, M.A.
Director of Education
Miller Intervention & Recovery Center
Olathe, KS

Janet Geringer Woititz, Ed.D.
Therapist, Private Practitioner
Upper Montclair, NJ
Author of *Adult Children of Alcoholics*

CONTENTS

1

Co-dependency: The Therapeutic Void

BY

SHARON   WEGSCHEIDER-CRUSE

Until just a few years ago, co-dependency was unknown in the alcoholism field. Treatment centers, dedicated to restoring the health and dignity of the alcoholic, ignored the needs of families (although there were a few programs designed to help spouses "understand their alcoholic"). Mental health professionals, even family counselors, somehow failed to isolate that specific class of behavioral symptoms that were common to families of alcoholics.

So co-dependency was caught in a therapeutic void between the alcoholism field and the mental health field, with the result that millions of people harbored feelings of craziness, fear of abandonment and a desperate need for love at the cost of personal dignity. They did so in pained silence and isolation.

Co-dependency is a primary disease and a disease within every member of an alcoholic family. It is what happens to family members when they try to adapt to a sick family system that seeks to protect and enable the alcoholic. Each family member enters into this collusion in his own individual way.

The spouse, for example, may learn controlling behavior by protecting the alcoholic from employers, the law and friends and extracting penance from him in the form of emotional subservience. This stimulates the alcoholic's feeling of low self-worth, which in turn tightens the control of the co-dependent. As that control progresses, the co-dependent becomes preoccupied with the alcoholic, upon whom she depends to feel needed.

Children fare no better in an alcoholic family. First, with their parents' example of intimacy and nurturance between adults, they grow up without the tools to establish joyful, healthy relationships. For them, *love = need = control;* and it is difficult, if not impossible, for adult children of alcoholics to surrender, to be vulnerable and to accept that it is okay to be wanted as opposed to being needed.

Second, as they grow into adulthood, children of alcoholics habituate behaviors which allowed them to function in their sick families, but which are self-destructive in the outside world. The successfully, compulsively achieving *family hero*, for example, was the rallying point around which the family staked its claim that it was a normal, healthy family. The hostile, rejecting *scapegoat* shunned the family and acted out his feelings in an attempt to get attention from a system that was already spread too thin. The *lost child* withdrew from the emotional chaos of family life in a seemingly benign way, but in fact, learned a cope-through-avoidance style which is devastating to the adult in terms of experiencing the richness of life. The *family mascot*, whose function was to provide comic relief for the family, learned to mask his most urgent communications ("love me, want me, accept me") with humor.

These behavioral types — these people — share at least two things:

1. They are hiding fear, shame and sadness.
2. Their rigidity precludes changing that.

I believe that the vicious cycle of co-dependency can only be stopped through intervention and professional care and that while co-dependency intervention is even more difficult than alcoholic intervention, it is absolutely necessary for a number of reasons:

1. A vast number of adult children of alcoholics either become alcoholics themselves, or marry them, thus recreating the harmful family system from which they came.
2. Children of alcoholics are highly prone to learning disabilities, eating disorders, stress-related medical problems and compulsive behaviors.
3. A childhood in which control skills and the suppression of feelings are necessary for survival can — and usually does — lead to an emotionally and spiritually impoverished adulthood.

We in the alcoholism field are not doing even half the job before us if we seek only to treat the alcoholic and return him/her to a co-dependent family system. Further, I would suggest that within a great many alcoholics lies an untreated co-dependent; and again, we have failed in our mandate if we arrest the alcoholism without recognizing the symptoms of co-dependency which led to the alcoholism to begin with. To fail in that is simply to create another "dry drunk".

Happily, our profession is on the cutting edge of making co-dependency a national issue, both on the social level and on the health level.

On the social level, I am especially proud of the National Association for Children of Alcoholics (NACoA), which was formed by an interdisciplinary team of therapists, teachers, authors and physicians who wish to serve as a network for co-dependents seeking support and help in their area, and who wish to see this country acknowledge its 28 million co-dependents.

On the level of public health, some large corporations across the country have taken the lead in establishing Employee Assistance Programs in which insurance benefits are extended to co-dependents.

We have come a long way from our perception of the sick, suffering, deluded, resisting alcoholic surrounded by his victimized family. There are many places where both can find separate, but equal treatment for their specific needs. But we are far from finished in bringing co-dependency to a satisfactory level of public awareness.

Continued success lies in education about the disease, its physical manifestations, its behavioral symptoms, and the role of the alcoholic in the recovery of the co-dependent. As Jael Greenleaf says, as long as the co-dependent is expected to play a role in the recovery of the alcoholics without the reverse being expected as well, the "sicker than thou" attitude on the part of the alcoholic may be perpetuated, which, in turn, perpetuates the "other-centeredness" that is so much a part of the disease of co-dependency.

2

Co-alcoholic/ Para-alcoholic: Who's Who?

BY

J A E L   G R E E N L E A F

Lhe growth of family treatment programs has given rise to new terminology and definitions of behavior to describe family members. However, the behavioral definitions of the entire family are often based primarily on the actions and attitudes of the spouse of the alcoholic. When the terms co-alcoholic and para-alcoholic are used interchangeably, that usage adds to the confusion about intra-family roles and their origins. This paper seeks to establish continuity in terminology and delineates the motives and origins of family member behavior by family role. The differences in the derivation of behavior of an adult in a volitional relationship with an alcoholic spouse and of a child

5

in a compulsory relationship with a parent are examined. Delineations of the adaptive response behaviors of children are presented and compared. The paper concludes that without these etiological distinctions, therapeutic treatment may result in an inappropriate assumption of responsibility and blame by the child. Finally, some barriers to effective treatment are explored.

Appropriate Terminology

With the increase in family programs, long-needed attention is being given to the children and spouses of alcoholic persons. As in any field, we need a common and consistent language in order to be understood by each other, the helping community, the media, and our clients. A consistent language aids us in distinguishing different aspects of the situation and interpreting the whole.

Separate terms present a continuation of the patterns in which the entire family becomes consumed by the alcoholic person's problem and identity.

As the Reverend Kellerman has observed, the medical model presents a very real problem to the family. Is alcoholism literally a family disease? Not unless everyone in the family has it. Alcoholism is an individual disease, but it is also a family syndrome. For this reason, I refer to the alcoholic person as the one having the disease and the other family members as the ones with the syndrome.

The prefix *co* means *with* or *necessary for the functioning of.* The adult who assists in maintaining the social and economic equilibrium of the alcoholic person is indeed co-alcoholic. These people take on responsibilities as the drinking escalates and the alcoholic person becomes increasingly impaired. For the family to continue to function with untreated alcoholism it is necessary for someone to step in and assume the responsibilities abandoned by the alcoholic member. Because the assumptive behavior maintains both the family and the alcoholism, that behavior is co-alcoholic.

The prefix *para* means *like* or *resembling.* The child who grows up in a family with the alcoholism syndrome learns behavior from both parents and becomes para-alcoholic.

That children imitate their parents is, of course, not news to anyone. The child sees and imitates both parents, not just the non-drinker. Invariably, the child will be rewarded for imitating both parents. For example, the child observes that the self-centered, uncooperative, destructive behavior of the alcoholic parent garners what the child longs for — attention. At the same time the child is pressured not to rock the boat, not to have needs or make demands. These paradoxical messages place the child in a "no win" position in which the imitation of both behaviors is sometimes rewarded and sometimes punished. These children have not lost their identities, they have never had the opportunity to form them. They become subject to situational reinforcement — also called people-pleasing. The paradox is carried out in their own behavior, which in some situations is alcoholic and in others is co-alcoholic. They themselves are neither; they are para-alcoholic.

In order to adequately distinguish between co-alcoholic and para-alcoholic behaviors, let us start at the beginning and examine their etiological differences.

Differential Etiology

The most immediate differences between the spouse of an alcoholic person and the child of an alcoholic parent are volition and mobility. Children have neither the choice nor the mobility to enter into or exit from the parent-child relationship. Put more simply, the adult may feel trapped; the child is trapped. The adult is intrapsychically helpless; the child is intrapsychically and situationally helpless.

This brings us to the most important etiological distinction: The adaptive response behavior of the adult versus the imitative response behavior of the child. The co-alcoholic adult came to the situation with a history of other situations. Adults learn that their responses to any given situation affect the outcome of that situation. It is this ability to effectively respond and produce results that is the essence of mastery and a sense of competence. Though this reservoir of effective responses may gradually become submerged as the co-alcoholic behavior develops, it nevertheless remains part of the adult's repertoire.

Children are not born with standards for evaluating behavior, social skills or moral values. They learn what they see and they do not learn what they do not see.

Thus, it is not enough to say that children are hurt by distorted parental behavior. We must ask what they see and what they do not see. What they do learn becomes the model not only for their own behavior, but for the choice of future relationships. What they do not learn will become apparent in their behavioral repertoire. Let us look at some specific behaviors, both co-alcoholic and para-alcoholic and the etiological differences between them.

Lying is part and parcel of the alcoholism syndrome. Spouses learn to live with lies and ultimately learn to tell them. They lie to cover up the alcoholism and to preserve family homeostasis. Their lying is goal-oriented and begins with both the awareness of falsehood and the intent to do good. Implicit in this are the pain and the guilt that always follow an abandonment of one's moral values. Lying is an adaptive response.

Children lie as well, often in grandiose fashion. And why not? There is no firm demarcation between the truth and the lie. Often the lie appears to be a greater value. They imitate the lying and simultaneously are deprived of a model for honesty. Often when confronted with their lies, they are genuinely bewildered, both by the disapproval and by the concept of truth for its own sake. They may lie to avoid the threat of unpleasantness or simply to relieve the drudgery of their reality. Their lying rarely induces guilt, since to them, there is nothing wrong with lying. In fact, they may be more likely to feel guilt telling the truth, if that truth reflects badly on someone important to them. To insist that the child "knows better" is a wholly unwarranted assumption and is received as a paradoxical message that creates culpability rather than honesty.

Depression, "the common cold of psychopathology", is endemic in families with the alcoholism syndrome. Co-alcoholic depression has its origin in loss. Loss of legitimate power, loss of dreams and expectations, loss of competence and self-esteem, loss of respect, loss of a shared goal, loss of friend and lover, and the agonizing loss of helplessly watching a loved one commit slow suicide. Overwhelming frustration and hurt give rise to chronic depression. Their depression is an adaptive response to a given stimulus.

Children's depression is different from spousal depression. There is depression that comes not from loss, but from deprivation. Numerous studies have been done on the effects of parental deprivation from infancy through adolescence. While the age of the child at the onset of deprivation is crucial and can mean the difference between reversible and irreversible damage, all of the studies demonstrate similar outcomes: depression, helplessness and hopelessness. Seligman, in his excellent research on learned helplessness, has called early childhood "the dance of development," and points out that when parents are focused elsewhere, there is no partner for the dance. Because the family with the alcoholic syndrome has altered its purpose from providing mutual support and caring to controlling the alcoholism, even the co-alcoholic parent is often unavailable or simply too exhausted and depressed to interact with the children. The child dances alone. Children learn that no one is there for them when they are in need. To assume that children's depression is based on a loss of self-esteem is to assume that self-esteem developed in the first place. Treatment plans for adults that are designed to restore previous feelings of self-worth may be inappropriate for children as construction plans that begin with the roof. To instruct them to behave "as if" is to reinforce an artifice that they already know too well and to deny the reality of their hurt, thus implying willful gain and culpability.

Denial is the common currency of troubled families. In families with the alcoholic syndrome, flattened effect, or the inability to display or express a full range of feelings, is almost invariable. Denial of the problem drinking requires denial of the problems that it causes. Concomitant with denial of the problem is denial of the feelings that the problems produce. This denial may have many origins, e.g., the suppression of anger to avoid a fight, the suppression of hope to avoid disappointment, the suppression of affection to avoid rejection. There are, I believe, two motivations for spouses to suppress their feelings. One is the reluctance to admit that the marriage is not working. There is a great deal of loss in that admission: loss of the wedding-day dream, loss of societal and parental approval, loss of self-esteem. To admit that the marriage is not working due to alcoholism is perceived by most spouses as not only failure, but personal failure. The feelings are seen as "wrong", because failure to maintain the marriage is wrong. By suppression of their feelings, they can deny externally the very thing that is so evident internally. Suppression conserves the illusion, but they are well aware that it is an illusion.

The second motivation is connected to the first. Suppressing feelings preserves the situation, for to fully acknowledge the loss, the anger, the frustration and the fear, would be to acknowledge necessity for change. The feelings are seen as "dangerous" because strong emotion is the impetus for action. When spouses suppress their feelings, they block their own actions.

Flattened effect in children is more complex. First of all, they do not have a model for the identification of a wide range of feelings. As parents suppress their feelings, they cease to discuss them and the children do not develop an adequate vocabulary of feeling words to describe their emotions. Feelings that cannot be named cannot be talked about.

As parents suppress their feelings, they cease to act on them or to display them. There is no model for appropriate emotional expression, and there is an implied negative judgment on the feelings themselves. Often, as the tension increases in the home, the implied judgment becomes overt. The child learns initially that expressing the feelings is wrong, and eventually, that having feelings is wrong.

The children suffer from both the absence of healthy emotional modeling and from punitive restrictions on their feelings. They repress their feelings in order to block other people's actions. To assume that these nice, well-behaved children do not feel the pain, rage and frustration that have been repressed is to perpetuate the rejection and denial under which they already labor. Such an attitude will continue to fill our clinics with children and adults who, when asked what they feel, will honestly answer "I don't know."

Lying, depression and flattened effect are only three of the behavioral symptoms exhibited by both co-alcoholic and para-alcoholic family members. I have discussed these three at length in order to give an idea of the importance of differential etiology in treatment design and implementation. Needless to say, there are many behaviors manifested by family members, and lengthy exploration of each one is beyond the scope of this paper. Therefore, I will present some of these behaviors in parallel columns with their etiological differences, as well as some behaviors that are uniquely para-alcoholic, but that I think are often misinterpreted.

This list could go on and on, but my purpose here is not to be exhaustive, but stimulating. Recognizing the etiological differences between co-alcoholic and para-alcoholic behavior is crucial in designing and implementing treatment programs for children (whether young or adult) from families with the alcoholism syndrome. Many of the distinctions may seem subtle, but if we return to the two basic roots of these distinctions we can readily see the importance of careful observation.

Children are not in the family by choice, nor can they leave; they are trapped and without resources. Adults are in the family only on their own volition — they may feel trapped and may ignore their resources, but the resources are still there. An eight-year-old child simply cannot say, "I don't like this any more, I'm going to get a job and move out."

Behavior or Set	Co-alcoholic	Para-alcoholic
Grandiosity	Often based on real assessment of task. A sort of martyred egotism at having done the work of two people.	Defense mechanism that is vital in preserving the nascent ego from collapse. Often based on fantasies of future success or revenge
Lack of trust	Disappointment in spouse often based on naive belief that spouse will or can be changed. Initial trust disintegrates.	Trust never develops, due to inconsistent, unpredictable parental behavior, lying, broken promises, etc. No visible model of trust. No comprehension of trust as value.
Blaming/Projecting	Fear of admission of "failure to make marriage work;" avoidance of responsibility for making change in own attitude/behavior.	Has never learned realistic consequences of behavior. Consequences often lacking altogether or extremely punitive. No adult model for taking responsibility. No model of separateness of boundaries.
Being Judgmental	Often attempts to assuage self-blame for failure of marriage. Stems from and perpetuates isolation.	Often attempt to "widen the target" of parental and self-blame, to find definition of good-bad. No model of forgiveness. Critical modeling.
Lying	Learn to live with lies, then begin to tell them. Aware of falsehood, intent to do good. Guilt inducing.	No model for discriminating between truth and lie. No concept of value of truth. Guilt is rare.
Depression	Based on loss, frustration, and "might have been."	1. Deprivation, helplessness, loneliness. 2. Assuming adult or parenting role without adult skill; role confusion. 3. Modeled addiction to depression.
Flattened effect	Stems largely from denial of drinking and problems. Avoiding loss of marriage ideal. Block own actions. Suppression.	Lack of feeling vocabulary. Re-action to negative judgment and/or direct reprimand. Reaction formation. Absence of healthy model. Model of flattened effect. Repression. Block other's actions.
Solitude	Anti-social, pathological withdrawal, selfish, snobbish.	Has become excessively reactive to others, thus unable to attend to own interests or relax if others are around. Solitude may be peaceful and constructive.
Disruptive	Hyperactive, acting-out, hostile, overly aggressive.	Has never seen logical consequences of own or parents behavior. Model of disruptive behavior. May be desperately seeking limits.

Children do not come to the family with fully developed personalities and years of adult experience with which to evaluate their own and their parents' behavior. They learn most (if not all) of their own behavior from their parents and cannot be made responsible for what they never learned to do. Adults have experience and other adults to whom they can turn for advice or commiseration. Their behavior is adaptive: that is, there were other behaviors operating before the alcoholism. Children do not have other behaviors operating — they are learning their behaviors at the moment.

An American may learn Chinese as an adaptive measure while living in China. The ability to speak English is retained and cannot only be used when necessary, but the opportunity to do so will probably be welcomed as comforting and familiar. If that American has a child while living in China and the only language that the child hears is Chinese, it should be no surprise when the child can only speak Chinese. Such a child will find the opportunity to speak English threatening and bewildering, rather than comforting or familiar. To insist that the child shape up on return to America and suddenly speak English is to indulge in the most cruel form of crazy-making.

So it is with para-alcoholic children. They grow up speaking a very strange language indeed, but it is the only one that they know. To insist that they suddenly speak "normic" is to pile crazy-making upon crazy-making.

Barriers to Effective Treatment

In order to provide appropriate and beneficial services to both the co-alcoholic and para-alcoholic person, we must begin by examining our attitudes that create barriers to effective treatment.

Almost invariably, treatment programs are primarily alcoholism treatment programs. Secondarily, there may be a spousal program, often justified solely by its value in enhancing the primary patient's sobriety. Rarely is there a program specifically designed for children. Usually, children are ignored, occasionally they are included in family groups, and infrequently there may be a play group for young children. Adult children are not treated at all. Thus, the alcoholism field replicates the alcoholic family system. The alcoholic is the center of attention, the co-alcoholic is viewed as either supporter or provoker, and the children are neglected. This situation short-changes not only the para- and co-alcoholic persons by depriving them of adequate treatment and full family support, it short-changes alcoholic persons by perpetuating the dichotomous position in which they are both isolated. Additionally, I believe that it is harmful to the alcoholic person's recovery because it maintains the character defect of false pride in being different, special and unique. It is harmful to the co- or para-alcoholic person's recovery because it perpetuates the other-centeredness so incompatible with true self-esteem.

The attitudinal barriers that stand specifically in the way of appropriate treatment for children are both pervasive and subtle.

The misuse of psychological or developmental assessment creates one of the largest and most insidious barriers to helping children. It (developmental assessment) is a method for observing subjects and organizing data; not making judgments. However, because we seek definitive answers, it becomes very tempting to make the often-subtle shift from evaluation to judgment. Tempting and very dangerous — dangerous because the erroneous conclusion often exacerbates the initial damage. The sequence goes something like this: the list of damages (non-constructive behaviors, negative attitudes, unpleasant traits, etc.) is developed and presented, e.g., Sandy is disruptive at home. If it stopped here, it would remain in relatively safe territory, but then the first error is made. The damages are tallied up to form a construct. Sandy is a disruptive child. It has become both individualized and conclusionary. The next step is to look for the reward or payoff for the behavior within the behavior itself. What does Sandy get from being disruptive? This produces the assumption that the response to a behavior is the same as the motivation for that behavior. When Sandy is disruptive, Sandy's parents argue with each other about how to handle the disruption, therefore Sandy's behavior seeks to provoke parental argument. Implicit in this is the assumption that non-constructive behavior both seeks and causes negative outcome. Sandy's behavior causes parental argument, therefore parental argument must be the payoff for Sandy. It sounds linear, sequential and logical, but this conclusion contains two extremely dangerous and destructive hypotheses: one, that children cause their parents' behavior and are therefore responsible for it; and two, that if that behavior is harmful, the children are somehow gratified by it.

Linear, sequential thinking does not necessarily lead to an accurate conclusion; logic often masquerades as the truth.

Children simply are not, were not and cannot be made culpable for situations in which adults abandon their responsibility. To deny this by doubletalking about their behavior as if it were malevolent is to perpetuate and to increase the blame that they already feel and to excuse adults from being adult.

It is an unfounded platitude that children are resilient. Not only is there no evidence to support this belief, but what evidence there is points in the other direction. The ability to bounce back into health from repeated or long-term psychological trauma requires a healthy, well-developed ego — which is not fully present until adulthood. When childhood development is consistently thwarted, one can only wonder just what they are to bounce back to.

A common phrase used to justify the denial of children's pain is: "she or he was too young to remember it anyway." Psychotherapeutic literature is filled with case histories in which repressed childhood trauma is the genesis of disordered behavior. When we say that children won't remember, what we really mean is that we hope that they won't remind us.

Treatment personnel, therapists, agency staff, parents, social workers, police, government officials, and all of us have one major thing in common: we are all adults. As such, we form an enormous and powerful peer group. One of the primary functions of any peer group, whether it is Hell's Angels or the United States Senate is to justify and validate each other's behaviors and mores. Thus, it becomes very easy to subscribe to the attitudes that insure our peer standing; in this case, that children are resilient, they won't be affected by what they cannot verbalize, or that they cause their parents' behavior. As we can all recall from adolescence, it is difficult and threatening to step outside of or to question the actions or beliefs of one's peer group. Taking that risk requires a resilient ego and substantial self-esteem.

All of the above barriers to treatment for children are also barriers to full, responsible adulthood when they are mechanistically recited in order to relieve parental or adult guilt.

While it is just and worthwhile to try to reduce guilt, it often becomes equated with reducing responsibility for children's recovery. This manifests as lack of services for children and incomplete recovery for adults. The 8th Step does not read "Made a list of all persons we had harmed and became willing to feel guilty about it." Guilt is the refuge of the self-centered, a refuge in which we can hide from responsibility. Consider the interior monologue of the guilt-ridden: "I was bad, I'm no good. No one likes me. No one respects me. I, I, me, me." Guilt requires no interaction with other people; it requires no action at all. Responsible action is the antithesis of guilt and the footwork of making amends. Making amends not only repairs damage, it cancels guilt and restores self-esteem. Making amends to children means providing treatment for them. Treatment that is based on their needs, not the agency's needs or the parent's needs.

Often, when children are included in treatment programs, they are put into groups with the co-alcoholic parent. This is inappropriate for several reasons.

1. As has been pointed out before, the etiology of their behavior is very different, yet such groups tend to address the development of co-alcoholic behavior only. Much of the format for co-alcoholic treatment is geared toward ending martyrdom: the "oh, poor me" innocent victim stance that adults use to perpetuate their self-imposed helplessness. Children, on the other hand, are innocent victims; their helplessness is not self-imposed, it is both situational and learned. Thus, the approach that is beneficial to the co-alcoholic parent is condemnatory to the child. It makes the very real pain and deprivaton that they suffer seem to be their own fault and they take on additional self-blame and inappropriate responsibility.

2. The inclusion of children inhibits the co-alcoholic parent from freely dealing with the difficulties of child-rearing. It may impose on them the demand to resolve their problems with their children before those problems have even been identified or defined.

3. Children, too, may feel inhibited about expressing their anger and hurt about the co-alcoholic parent's behavior. The majority of children in Margaret Cork's study felt rejected and neglected by the non-alcoholic parent as well as the alcoholic parent. This has been borne out in my own observations as well. In interviews with adult children, I have asked this question: "Remember yourself as a child needing solace or emotional support. Both parents are available and the alcoholic parent is neither drunk nor hungover. To whom would you turn?" The answer almost invariably was the alcoholic parent, not the co-alcoholic parent. The only consistent exception to this was if the alcoholic parent was physically abusive. In that case, the answer was usually "neither one".

Perhaps we should stop thinking of these people as "children of alcoholics". Children have two parents, not one. They are children of co-alcoholic parents as well and need treatment, even if the alcoholic parent has been out of the family for a long time.

4. The lumping together of spouses and children perpetuates the we-they dichotomy that is in itself a barrier to full reconciliation.

There is one barrier to children's services that can be turned into an advantage. Para-alcoholic persons grow up and go into social service work like lemmings go into the sea. If they are still in denial about their own need for recovery, they may deny the need for treating children. Without recovery, they may be a serious barrier to appropriate services; with recovery, they can be a tremendous asset. If we believe in the peer approach, we must have staff members who work primary co-alcoholic and para-alcoholic recovery programs (primary meaning persons who are not also alcoholic). If we believe that the five most important words in recovery are, "I know how you feel," then we must have people who can honestly say them. Once again, we come down to what always seems to be the biggest barrier in anything having to do with alcoholism. Whether it is getting the alcoholic person into treatment or abolishing the stigma of alcoholism, the highest hurdle is always denial. This time, however, it's not theirs, it's ours.

Conclusion

To break through our own denial, we must begin to look at the treatment of the alcoholic person as a means, not an end. A program that treats only the person with the disease of alcoholism and not those within the alcoholism syndrome is comparable to a garage that specializes in changing only right front tires and not the other three.

Para-alcoholic and co-alcoholic members have been ignored by the alcoholism field and misunderstood by the mental health field. It was only when alcoholism was differentiated from the mental illness and other diseases that adequate and effective services began to emerge. Adequate and effective services for co-alcoholic and para-alcoholic persons depend on the same kind of differentiation. In order to clarify and understand these separate problems, we need clear, consistent and appropriate terminology. We cannot talk about something vaguely, saying that it is sort of like something else and hope to develop specific treatment programs.

We need people. We need people like Sharon Wegscheider-Cruse, Janet Woititz, Margaret Cork and Claudia Black, whose research and writing have helped us to understand the roles and the reality within the family. We need more pioneering people to start Adult Children of Alcoholics meetings across the country.

Most of all, we need ourselves. If we do not provide adequate services for children, they will not go away. They will simply grow up and keep alcoholism treatment programs in business. Perhaps, some day, someone in one of those programs will wonder why there are so many clients with the same last name.

3

Co-dependent Relationships

BY

K A T H Y   C A P E L L — S O W D E R

Stanton Peele, in *The Addiction Experience,* describes addiction as "a lifestyle, a way of coping with the world and ourselves, a way of interpreting our experience . . ." Don Wegscheider in *If Only My Family Understood Me* defines addiction as "a progressive focusing of all attention on a target — an activity which preempts the expression of one's feelings." While it is commonly accepted that addiction to alcohol and drugs exists, it is less commonly understood that the person involved in a primary love relationship with someone addicted, frequently displays symptoms of addiction him/herself in the ways that he/she relates to the relationship. This chapter will attempt to make this relationship clear and to help co-dependents define their own symptoms and clarify means by which they can establish their own recovery programs. (Note: For purposes of this chapter, the alcoholic will be referred to as "he"; the co-dependents as "she" or "spouse".)

In order to parallel the symptomatology of co-dependent addiction to alcohol and drug addiction, it is important to review the symptoms of addiction. An alcoholic becomes increasingly preoccupied with getting and using alcohol to the degree that his lifestyle is centered around its use. He protects his supply, and in so doing, compromises and breaks his value systems, resulting in guilt, self-hatred, and loss of self-esteem. He drinks or uses more, needing more of his chemical to gain relief, achieving an increasingly higher tolerance. Meanwhile, his major life areas are spiraling downward (e.g., family relationships, friends, job, health, finances), despite his insistence that he has no problem with alcohol or drugs. He continues to deny his loss of control despite increasing evidence to the contrary. He continues to seek the old "highs", but gradually loses the ability to feel the euphoria of earlier days, now drinking or using in an attempt to feel normal. When the addiction process is "broken", usually by some form of crisis, the addict often experiences physical signs of withdrawal, as well as emotional withdrawal, similar to the grief process experienced as a result of the loss of a loved one.

As the alcoholic becomes increasingly preoccupied with getting, using and keeping the alcohol, the "developing co-dependent" becomes more focused on that person, his behavior, and his chemical use, and begins to change her own behavior in response to the alcoholic's lifestyle. Behavior changes may include efforts to check on or control the drinking or drinking-related friends or activities ("protecting her supply"), peacekeeping within the family system, isolation from activities outside the family, basically adding up to focusing on the drinker himself (the definition of addiction), and a lifestyle centered around him.

As the alcoholic loses control of the amounts and frequency of his drinking, the co-dependent naturally loses more control of the drinker and his behavior, and as the alcoholic's tolerance for alcohol increases, the co-dependent hangs on more compulsively to her defenses, however unconscious, designed to control the drinker and his responses. Therefore, she, too, is in essence building an "increase in tolerance" to unacceptable behavior from the drinker (one characteristic of enabling), and losing control, not only of the drinker's responses, but her own emotions, mood-swings and reactions. In response to the deterioration of this primary relationship and the alcoholic's denial that his drinking and behavior is a problem, she begins to accept projected blame and questions her own self-worth and adequacy. In essence, she gives the alcoholic the power to determine her reactions, feelings, moods, much as the alcoholic does his alcohol. She builds defenses for surviving in the relationship and the family system, and for protecting herself from the pain (e.g., repression, taking responsibility for others, acting happy and "all together," self righteousness). As she gains temporary relief from use of these defenses (like the alcoholic gains relief from drinking), she uses them more frequently and habitually, although usually unconsciously. So as the alcoholic numbs his painful feelings with alcohol and other defenses (e.g., projection, blaming, aggressive behaviors), the co-dependent also anesthetizes her pain with natural defenses in a progressively numbing process. As her addiction progresses, she, too, is in denial that she is as affected by the drinking lifestyle as he is. More often, her concern is for the drinker or the effects she sees on her children. Even then, her picture of reality is often distorted and minimized.

As the co-dependent's needs are met less frequently or in less healthy ways, she often compromises her value system (as the drinker does in efforts to obtain and protect his chemical, his declining self-image, or in his states of intoxication and lowered inhibitions). In her case, she may have an affair, she may abuse or neglect the children; she may abandon spiritual beliefs, or she may lie about her own activities or his behavior outside of the immediate family, all of which contribute to her own self-hatred and loss of self-respect.

As her addiction progresses, her major life areas decline, as do the drinker's. Her first area affected is emotional, with increasing self-doubts, feelings blunted with defenses and grief over the loss of a love relationship, to name a few; closely related is often a change in sexual response. She is usually affected socially, often isolating herself from old friends and activities, due to loss of interest, attempts to avoid anticipated disapproval, or desire to keep an eye on the drinker. Her family is affected, her children often becoming protective and caretaking of her needs, or resentful of her controlling, overprotectiveness and dominance though often they are unaware of or do not talk about these effects. Her spiritual life often suffers, resulting in her feeling abandoned by or non-deserving of God. Physically, she often experiences stress-related problems such as chronic headaches, backaches or gastrointestinal disorders. These can impact on her job performance through loss of efficiency, frequent absences or hospitalizations. Or her job function may take the other extreme of workaholism, which may be a form of withdrawing from the home situation and gaining self-esteem through work achievement. Another area affecting both the alcoholic and the co-dependent spouse is the loss of volition. As the drinker loses the power of choice over his consumption of alcohol, and resulting behaviors, the co-dependent loses the ability to see her options or to take action on them. Therefore, she feels trapped in the "victim's role", unable to see her own enabling behaviors or the power she is giving up.

As these symptoms of addiction progress, often she begins to plan her escape. This may take the form of hoarding money, saving for the day when the children leave home, or it may take the form of separation, divorce or even suicide. When an actual breakup in the relationship occurs, the co-dependent spouse experiences a form of withdrawal, often losing her appetite, becoming restless or lethargic, having difficulty sleeping and experiencing feelings of disorientation. Often the breakup is shortlived, despite no real resolution of differences, similar to the alcoholic's drinking to ward off withdrawal. Often there is a "hanging on" to the relationship despite no conscious gains for the co-dependent or no realistic basis for hope or change; perhaps this parallels the alcoholic's continuing to drink in an effort to "regain the old highs".

It is an often-noted phenomenon that the alcoholic becomes addicted to other things (gambling, workaholism, etc.), even after sobriety. The co-dependent, too, often develops addictions in other areas, such as compulsive eating, spending and not infrequently, becomes alcoholic or drug dependent (commonly on prescribed tranquilizers) herself. Though she may ultimately sever her ties to this alcoholic marriage, she is likely to become involved with another alcoholic or addictive relationship, carry her own addictive symptoms into new relationships, as well as her child-rearing practices, perpetuating the cycle further into new generations.

A co-dependent, like an alcoholic, denies her own addictive symptoms. Her denial often takes the form of thinking that once she breaks off from the alcoholic relationship, she will be fine. She fails to see how she carries her addictive thinking, responses and behaviors into other areas of her life, and denies the need for her own treatment.

The first step of recovery must be to help her break through her own denial and to become aware of the compulsiveness of her own defenses. Overcoming addiction is as much building positive involvements in one's environment as it is withdrawing from addictive attachments.

CHARACTERISTICS

Love (Open System)

Room to grow, expand; desire for other to grow.

Addiction (Closed System)

Dependent, based on security and comfort; use intensity of need and infatuation as proof of love (may really be fear, insecurity, loneliness).

Love (Open System)	Addiction (Closed System)
Separate interests; other friends; maintain other meaningful relationships.	Total involvement; limited social life; neglect old friends, interests.
Encouragement of each other's expanding; secure in own worth.	Preoccupation with other's behavior; dependent on other's approval for own identity and self-worth.
Trust; openness.	Jealousy, possessiveness (fears competition) "protects supply."
Mutual integrity preserved.	One partner's needs suspended for the other's; self-deprivation.
Willingness to risk and be real.	Search for perfect invulnerability — eliminates possible risks.
Room for exploration of feelings in and of relationship.	Reassurance through repeated, ritualized activity.
Ability to enjoy being alone.	Intolerance — unable to endure separations (even in conflict); hang on even tighter. Undergo withdrawal — loss of appetite, restless, lethargic, disoriented agony.

BREAKUPS

Accept breakup without feeling a loss of own adequacy and self-worth.	Feel inadequate; worthless. Often unilateral decision.
Wants best for partner, though apart; can become friends.	Violent ending — often hate other; try to inflict pain. Manipulation to get other back.

ONE-SIDED ADDICTION

	Denial, fantasy; (overestimation of other's commitment).
	Seeks solutions outside ourselves — drugs, alcohol, new lover, change of situation.

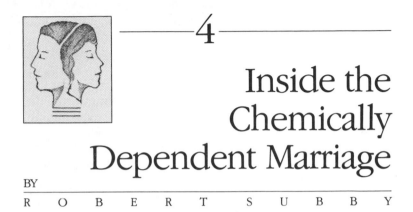

4

Inside the Chemically Dependent Marriage

BY

R   O   B   E   R   T   S   U   B   B   Y

What I think most of us have a struggle with in this field of chemical dependency, especially in our early recoveries, is that we, ourselves, have not yet addressed some of our own unfinished, co-dependent family issues. As a result, we haven't crossed over our own developmental boundary of intra- and interpersonal mistrust. We may also not yet have built a community of people who understand us and all that we feel.

When it comes right down to reaching inside ourselves or having someone hug us, we become paralyzed. I know that as a recovering co-dependent alcoholic, I had conned my way through the better part of my life. I didn't realize during the early years of recovery that

I had to give that neglected child inside me permission to talk about his feelings. I didn't know how important this was in order to learn how to trust.

While the average person might recognize that the alcoholic, the co-dependent or the child of an alcoholic is not being honest, the affected individual cannot see this. For him, the need to protect himself through his manipulation of the truth is a sincere one. The experiences that first taught the co-dependent to deny, minimize, or alter the truth are usually linked to his early childhood.

Fear of judgment by others and ultimate rejection is a powerful force that operates in his life. Before these people can hope to build a meaningful relationship with another person, they must first go back and retrieve the child inside them who was stunted in his emotional growth. It's always a kind of push and pull experience for these co-dependent adult children. They need others and seek to get their needs met, but lack trust, and so are unable to risk letting others in.

Earlier on in my work, I saw co-dependency only as a reactive and compulsive pattern of those family members who were struggling to separate themselves from the emotional pain that accompanied their living with a practicing alcoholic more recently, I have come to understand co-dependency as a condition which for many individuals, long preceded their experiences with active alcoholism. Today I define co-dependency as:

An emotional psychological and behavioral condition that develops as a result of an individual's prolonged exposure to, and practice of, a set of oppressive rules — rules which prevent the open expression of feeling as well as the direct discussion of personal and interpersonal problems.

I don't know if the term co-dependency will still be in use 10 or 15 years from now, but for today I know of no other satisfactory term. My only struggle with the word co-dependency is that currently it seems linked solely to the issue of alcoholism, and I would like to see that change. I would like to have alcoholism viewed as only one of many unhealthy realities which co-dependency might foster.

Co-dependency, as I stated before, is an emotional psychological and behavioral pattern of coping that is born of the rules of a family and not as a result of alcoholism. In the way of review, these rules include: we don't talk about how we feel, we don't talk about our problems, and we do not rock the boat. Co-dependency is a condition which precedes the alcoholic experience. In essence, it is the practice of oppressive rules within the family which support compulsive-obsessive behavior patterns such as alcoholism, overeating, overworking and perfectionism.

Now, having set the developmental stage for co-dependency, I would like to talk a bit about the serious abyss which develops between the individual's emotional, spiritual and psychological selves.

There is a private logic that co-dependents develop in order to cope. The co-dependent individual goes out and seeks a partner and, as I mentioned earlier, seems destined to find a partner who lives by a set of rules similar to his own. Once the novelty of these superficial relationships wears off and they fall into the developmental void with which they have both lived as a result of their co-dependent histories, the marriage begins to falter. They fight about sex, money, work, the kids; but as good co-dependents, they skillfully avoid their feelings. These other issues serve to keep the focus off their relationship and the emotional pain that surrounds them. The couple may eventually seek a divorce because they can't find the intimacy they are looking for.

The children of these troubled marriages begin to act out in an effort to get Mom and Dad back together. Mom has to talk to Dad and Dad has to talk to Mom. The children don't always understand at a conscious level what they are doing, but they do feel early on that they are being asked to take care of their parents. This is a horrendous responsibility for a child to take on, but they do it.

The co-dependent children become the therapists for their troubled parents. As a co-dependent child myself, I knew how to play therapist long before I had ever received any professional training.

These inappropriate role behaviors on the part of the children are early signs of what will eventually become their own adult co-dependency struggle.

Unarrested, the co-dependent couple may try having another child to bring them back together. When this fails, the couple may try a geographic escape or a different job. Perhaps one of the partners may decide that an affair would help. These are medicative approaches to recovery that serve only to postpone the inevitable; their need to face themselves and their own histories.

When you can't talk about your feelings, you are forced to project your feelings away from yourself, and the message early on in the alcoholic family is to develop this kind of maladaptive behavior just to survive emotionally. Because of the implicit and explicit messages that you're not okay, life inside the sick family is a no-trust experience, and the bottom line is shame. Guilt is being able to say to yourself, "I did something wrong. I broke the rules." Shame, on the other hand, is when you look inside yourself and say, "I am wrong. I am no good. I am insufficient. I am not adequate." So we begin to get in touch with that shame as children and that hurts.

The psychology of a child is always to rebel away from pain. If you put your hand on a hot burner once, you probably won't do it again. Similarly, when the child feels his shame message go off, he tends to orchestrate his life in such a way so as to make sure that he will never have to feel that pain again. Inside, alone, there is only me depending on me; and me saying to you whenever you try to tell me what to do, "Nobody knows better than me."

When the co-dependent is confronted on his or her behavior, there is a strong possibility that they will fall into their shame. The result is a predictable knee-jerk reaction.

The co-dependent spouse seeks approval from his partner like the co-dependent child seeks approval from his parent. Try as they might, *the partners of a co-dependent marriage fail for the simple reason that a husband can't be a father to his wife, and a wife can't be a mother to her husband.* The co-dependent couple cannot see this reality and so end up punishing each other for what they perceive as their spouse's fault to be there for them.

Someone once told me that true intimacy never demands of another human being what they would not freely give. In treating the co-dependent marriage, it is extremely important that the therapist be able to break away from the traditional concepts of marriage counseling and return to the needs of the individuals living within the marriage.

Once the individual establishes a relationship of trust within the clinical setting, he or she can begin to address the underlying issues of shame and guilt which divide them. Reconstruction of these early developmental issues, metaphorically speaking, requires that the co-dependent go back and retrieve the child within. This concept of divided self is, I believe, a vital issue in the treatment of co-dependency. The hallmark of this disease is the division between our emotional and spiritual selves. I don't think that co-dependency is a phenomenon unique to the members of the alcoholic family. This, to me, is an extremely important point to bring out.

I believe that the emerging concept of co-dependency may offer a theoretical bridge by which the mental health, family therapy and chemical dependency fields might come together. I would hate to see us miss this opportunity as helping professionals. Our collective challenge as mental health and chemical dependency practitioners is also to recognize the significance of these unfinished issues in our own lives, and how they may prevent us from being truly open to our clients.

5

Co-dependency

BY

R O B E R T   S U B B Y   A N D   J O H N   F R I E L

C o-dependency is a term that has been widely used within the chemical dependency field over the past several years, but it is often misunderstood. Originally, it was used to describe the person or persons whose lives were affected as a result of their being involved with someone who was chemically dependent. The "co-dependent" spouse or child or lover of someone who was chemically dependent was seen as having developed a pattern of coping with life that was not healthy, as a reaction to someone else's drug or alcohol abuse. The now-familiar strategies of minimizing problems or of total denial of problems was seen as a reaction to the chemically dependent person's maladaptive behavior, and we will include this type of co-dependency in our discussion. But what many professionals are coming to realize is that these co-dependent patterns of coping do not necessarily develop solely as a result of having lived with a chemically dependent person. In fact, through specific research and clinical work on family systems, it is now becoming clearer that co-dependency is a condition which can emerge from any family system where certain unwritten, even unspoken, rules exist. These unwritten family rules and their effect on our approach to living form the focus of this chapter.

Let us define co-dependency, then, as a dysfunctional pattern of living and problem-solving which is nurtured by a set of rules within the family system. These rules make healthy growth and change very difficult. For the reader who is not familiar with the concept of co-dependency, we have listed some of the common characteristics below:

1. Difficulty in actually identifying feelings — Am I angry? Am I lonely? Am I sad? Do I feel hurt? Or what?
2. Difficulty expressing feelings — I am feeling hurt. But how might others act toward me if they knew how I feel? And worse, what might they think of me if they knew my true feelings?
3. Difficulty in forming or maintaining close relationships — I want to be close to others, but I am afraid of being hurt or rejected by them.
4. Perfectionism — too many expectations for self and others.
5. Rigid or stuck in attitudes and behavior — even though it hurts to live this way, it's the only way I know.
6. Difficulty adjusting to change.
7. Feeling overly responsible for other people's behavior or feelings — I am embarrassed by what someone else does.
8. Constant need for other's approval in order to feel good about self.
9. Difficulty making decisions — worrying or thinking so much that you get "stuck".
10. General feelings of powerlessness over one's life — nothing I do makes any difference.
11. A basic sense of shame and low self-esteem over perceived failures in one's life.

Because many co-dependent people appear to be so self-sufficient, "strong" and in control of their lives, Friel (1982) has also termed this pattern "paradoxical dependency", the paradox being that beneath the public image of strength and security often lie the opposite feelings of insecurity, self-doubt and confusion. "Everyone thinks I am so strong, and all of my friends and relatives come to me with their problems," say many co-dependent people, "but if they knew the real me, they would be very surprised. Sometimes it's all I can do just to get through each day." How does this happen? How do we get to this point where who we really are and who everyone thinks we are, are so different? How do we learn to live this way? According to Subby, the co-dependent learns to do only those things which will get him the approval and acceptance of others. By doing this, unfortunately, he gradually denies much of who he really is. The drawings below will help to illustrate how this denial process looks for the co-dependent

Figure 5-1. Growth of Co-dependent.

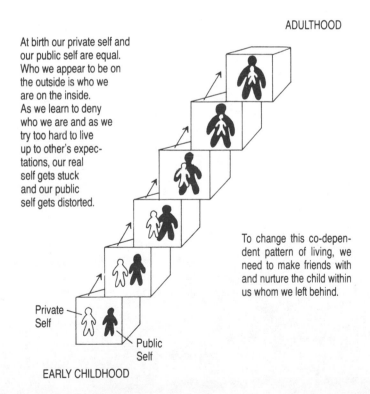

ADULTHOOD

At birth our private self and our public self are equal. Who we appear to be on the outside is who we are on the inside. As we learn to deny who we are and as we try too hard to live up to other's expectations, our real self gets stuck and our public self gets distorted.

To change this co-dependent pattern of living, we need to make friends with and nurture the child within us whom we left behind.

Private Self

Public Self

EARLY CHILDHOOD

In our view, these patterns of living develop through practice. By practicing a set of rules which we learn as we are growing up, or in some cases, after we have grown up, we become co-dependent in our way of living. When we say that co-dependency originates in the family system, we mean that some — or all — of the characteristics listed above are transmitted to family members through a set of rules.

Let's look at perfectionism for a moment. It is okay to expect things to be done correctly most of the time. We try to put the garbage in the garbage can, for example, rather than putting it out on the lawn. But we see many people being downright unhappy because they expect every minor detail to go exactly as they had planned. And when we grow up in perfectionistic families, we tend to become perfectionistic, too, because it's all we know. When Dad yells and screams about a thousand little things, Mom and Dad yell at each other for minor household tasks left undone, then we begin to believe that it is very bad to leave minor things around the house undone. In fact, we eventually begin to believe that each little mistake that we make in life is a major tragedy. In extreme cases, it's not too long before we begin saying to ourselves over and over, "If only I hadn't been born. If only I were smarter or prettier or more athletic or more, more something, then everything would be okay." It's hard to feel good about ourselves when we judge everything we do as not measuring up to someone else's standards.

Basically, how we treat ourselves and others is a direct result of the rules that we learned to follow as we were growing up. How we handle things like stress and conflict as adults is the result of how we learned to handle them as kids. How we choose to handle them in the present is up to us. Let's examine some of these rules which keep us stuck in co-dependent patterns of living.

1. It's not okay to talk about problems.
2. Feelings should not be expressed openly.
3. Communication is best if indirect, with one person acting as messenger between two others (triangulation).
4. Unrealistic expectations — be strong, good, right, perfect. Make us proud.
5. Don't be "selfish".
6. Do as I say, not as I do.
7. It's not okay to play or be playful.
8. Don't rock the boat.

If you look more carefully at these rules, you will begin to see that they all have something to do with protecting or isolating oneself from others by not taking the risk to get close. People growing up according to these rules don't realize that there are actually many families that do allow each individual to talk about problems outside the family, or to express emotions openly, or to make mistakes without undue criticism. They don't realize that in many families, being vulnerable and asking for help is both routine and okay. That isolating and denying oneself is not the best way to be.

Two Examples

At 13, Jim was an average student, attractive, popular among his peers, athletic and extroverted, but because his father was an alcoholic, Jim lived two lives. At home he was lonely and terrified over what others might find out about his family. Jim was depressed, filled with shame and doubt, guilty for wrongs and never committed, and deeply resentful. Unable to discuss the fear, anger or any of the other normal emotions he was feeling, Jim turned to alcohol and drugs.

Twelve years later, Jim entered treatment for chemical dependency, where for the first time he learned that the family rules operating while he was growing up were largely responsible for his inability to face his own personal problems constructively. In an effort to compensate for these unhealthy rules, Jim had developed a pattern of perfectionism, compulsive overworking, and destructive dependency in his interpersonal relationships, in addition to his alcoholism.

Anne was 10 when she started to withdraw into the safety of her own private fantasy world. An excellent student, shy, eager to please and inhibited, Anne began to develop a pattern of compulsive overeating, televison-viewing and studying. Beneath it all she was fearful, anxious, lonely and depressed. Although neither her parents nor any of her close friends were chemically dependent, the therapist whom she saw first many years later recognized her compulsive, approval-seeking, dependent behavior patterns and referred her to an outpatient co-dependency treatment program.

During treatment, Anne discovered for the first time that her problems were rooted in the same set of family rules which led to

Jim's chemical dependency. Both Jim and Anne came from families in which there was a "no talk" rule, in which communication was poor, in which outward expressions of emotions were discouraged, in which personal identity and needs came second, and in which they always fell short of their parents' expectations. Unable to face the difficult tasks of growing up, both Jim and Anne were forced to develop these unhealthy patterns of coping.

While Jim became chemically dependent, and Anne became co-dependent as a result of their respective backgrounds, the fact of the matter is that given the set of rules listed above, we can expect many people coming out of these family systems to be either chemically dependent, or co-dependent, or both.

The Rules In Detail

Rule 1. It's not okay to talk about problems.

How do we learn this rule? In some families, it's easy to see how. Everyone tells you, "Don't air your dirty laundry in public." "Now, Suzy, I don't want you running over to the neighbor's house and telling them all of our business," etc. In other families the message is just as strong without being spoken. For example, you never hear Mom and Dad talk about problems, although you see and feel the tension sometimes. You notice the occasional glare, or feelings of walking on eggshells that occur in any family when conflict arises, but no one ever says anything. It's not long before you realize that if you want to fit in and be like Mom and Dad, then it's probably best not to talk about problems. Or when a difficult topic arises, everyone just sort of disappears, or gets quiet, distracted by television, leaving a cloud of tension hanging in the air.

How does adherence to this rule affect us? It eventually makes us avoid our own problems, deny that we have any problems, and contrary to what you might think, it fosters a sense of impending doom much of the time, typified by knots in the stomach, free-floating anxiety, headaches and sleeplessness . . . to name a few. It makes us numb in all kinds of ways. Since we aren't supposed to talk about problems, we begin to believe that if we admit having problems, then there will be something horribly wrong with us that is not wrong with most people. If we admit to having a problem, then we fear that we will also be judged by others as weak and unhealthy. Ultimately, this results in a deep sense of shame about a very real part of every-day life . . . i.e., that we all have problems. And, of course, as you might expect, it is impossible to solve a problem if you don't know how to talk about it, or even acknowledge that you have one. This perhaps is the most frustrating, saddening outcome of the "no-talk" rule.

Rule 2. Feelings are not expressed openly.

In the first place, we Americans are known for being a bit inhibited when it comes to showing our feelings. We like the image of being clever and practical. We take pride in being able to hide our emotions and solve all our problems without help. We can put a man on the moon, design and build sophisticated structures, replace diseased organs, even give back someone their sight, but when it comes to expressing our true feelings, we are often like a fish out of water.

In families with unresolved chemical and co-depndency issues, this emotional blocking is an even greater problem. Expressing feelings is hard enough, but especially so when the spoken or unspoken rules make it clear that we just "don't". Statements like "big boys don't cry," or "I'll give you something to cry about," are obvious ways that this rule is learned. But there are more subtle ways. For example, when a child, feeling frightened or lonely, tries to sit on his father's lap or give him a hug, Dad gets tense. He may not say anything, but his back may arch a little and his shoulders stiffen. The father in this case might be uncomfortable with his own feelings, and as a result, may end up conveying this discomfort to his child. In time, the child might learn not to show his feelings around Dad at all.

The results of not expressing our feelings are many. We may come to believe that it is better to deny what we feel, rather than to risk letting someone else see who we really are inside. Eventually, this cutting off of our emotional selves becomes so complete that, indeed, even we do not know who we really are. Our heads tell us one thing, like we don't care what others think or say, while our bodies unconsciously begin to tell us something else. We develop things like tension headaches or migraines, ulcers, hypertension, rashes, loss of sleep or sleeping too much, depression or anxiety. and because we are now so cut off from our feelings, we don't see how they are affecting us.

Rule 3. Communcation is often indirect, with one person acting as messenger between two others (triangulation).

Dad says to Tom, age 14, "I wish you'd tell your mother to be more understanding of me. She's really being grouchy lately. She doesn't know how much it hurts me." Tom goes away thinking that he can really fix things up if he lets Mom know the "inside scoop" on how Dad really feels. Tom says to Mom, "You know, Mom, Dad has been feeling pretty down lately about the way you've been reacting to him . . ."

What's so unusual about this scene? Isn't it fairly common? Isn't it part of family togetherness to include children in our lives? Perhaps it is, but not in this way. Using a messenger this way, whether a child or an adult, can make things awfully confusing. First, Tom gets caught in the middle. If he doesn't tell Mom, then he lets Dad down. If he does tell her, he risks receiving the anger or rejection from Mom that she's really directing toward Dad. And in either case, both Mom and Dad are using Tom to avoid talking face-to-face as adults. If used on a regular basis, this kind of communication pattern can make everyone extremely sick and upset inside. Messages get mixed or confused, feelings get misdirected and innocent people become victims of others' inability to confront personal problems directly. The pain can become unbearable.

Rule 4. Unrealistic expectations: be strong, good, right, perfect. Make us proud.

Doing well and achieving is important to most of us. And most of us have a fairly clear idea of how we think things should be done or handled. Sometimes, though, we begin to believe that there is only one right way. What's worse, we begin to believe that enough is never enough. There is only one Albert Einstein, only one Willie Mays, only one Eleanor Roosevelt, and only one Madam Curie. Your child or spouse cannot, therefore, become Albert Einstein or Madam Curie. And, besides, those people were not perfect and certainly they would be the first to admit that fact.

What happens in some families is that we create an ideal in our heads about what is good or right or best, and this ideal is so far removed from what is possible and realistic that we wind up punishing others because they do not meet our expectations. We begin to nag and push and criticize and analyze and cajole. We become deeply disappointed with those who don't meet our expectations. Then we begin to blame ourselves for not pushing others enough to meet our expectations, and pretty soon everyone is unhappy . . . me, you and those who have to watch what is going on between us. Live and let live is perhaps the most difficult principle for us to live by.

Rule 5. Don't be selfish.

For the co-dependent who grows up in the system where this rule is rigidly applied to every situation, feelings of guilt are certain to emerge. They learn to view themselves as wrong for placing their own needs before the needs of others. The idea that a person is being selfish for thinking of himself first is totally unrealistic. Normally there are times in life when it makes good sense to take care of your own needs first. A politician votes for himself because he believes he is the best man for the job. The co-dependent goes into counseling, risking the rejections of an alcoholic spouse because he/she knows that help is needed.

If we believe that our own needs are wrong, we will never be able to get those needs met. What often happens in co-dependency is that we try to feel good about ourselves by taking care of others and eventually our self-esteem becomes dependent on caretaking. Without someone to take care of, the co-dependent is left with no purpose or worth. The more we take care of someone, the more we fail to take care of our own needs. In time, we start to feel resentful toward those whom we care for because they fail to recognize what we are doing for them. The result of these angry feelings is that we experience even more shame, and so we try harder than ever to make up for it by doing even more caretaking. The co-dependent spouse, the child of the alcoholic and the chemically dependent person all suffer as a result of this taking-care-of behavior. As the pain builds in each of us, we begin to blame and point out the failings of others. We become sarcastic, crabby, angry, and pessimistic, because we feel that everyone is taking from us and giving nothing in return. Ultimately, this circular pattern becomes like an emotional merry-go-round that keeps getting worse as time goes on. The way out of this cycle is to look at it in a paradoxical way. To break the painful hold that this "don't be selfish" rule has on the co-dependent, he must first decide to be "selfish" and take care of himself. This means that in order to get free, the individual must first stop the very thing that he has come to believe will earn him the acceptance and love which he needs. When the co-dependent discovers that taking care of himself first is often the best way to be of help to others and gain their respect, he will also find self-respect. In other words, while the risk to change is a difficult one at first, in the long run the rewards for taking the risk are great.

Rule 6. Do as I say . . . not as I do.

This rule, perhaps more than any other, teaches us not to trust. If, as children, our parents tell us to be honest, and then turn right around and tell a lie, we become confused. We become suspicious. We stop taking risks and count only on ourselves. We do this out of a need to protect ourselves from the pain of inconsistency. Remember the time that Dad promised to take you to the movies or fishing on Saturday afternoon, but instead decided to play golf; or maybe he had to work, or worst of all, he started to drink. After a few disappointments like this one, we start to wonder whether or not our parents love us and whether we count. Many of us who experience these inconsistencies of the "Do as I say, not as I do" rule, came to believe as children, that we really aren't good enough and don't deserve our parents' love. Unable to get our parents' approval, we seek out new ways of getting attention. Conscious or otherwise, our goal is to manipulate others to give us validation and love. Who we are inside is not good enough or deserving enough, so we hide this unacceptable part and learn to do those things which will bring us approval from others. The most destructive part of this particular rule is that by doing only what we think others want us to do, we deny ourselves and become divided inside. Denying who we really are prevents us from ever knowing if those people close to us really care about us or love us. After all, we have only let them know that part of us which we believed they would accept. We live in constant fear of being rejected if they should ever find out the truth. Trying to do the "right" thing does not make us secure, because we are not being true to ourselves. We know a lot about the truth as a result of trying to avoid it, but we never feel okay.

Rule 7. It's not okay to play.

From the very beginning, the co-dependent person believes that the world is a very serious place. Life is difficult and always painful. Like all of the rules previously mentioned, this rule lends itself to the development of a co-dependent view of ourselves as unlovable, boring, stupid, ugly and wrong. Because of this, the co-dependent must work twice as hard as everyone else just to feel okay. Believing that what they do is who they are, it becomes increasingly important to their feeling okay that they not be without something to do. It's okay to play if you are a child, but not if you are an adult. The longer we deny our need to play, the more we suffer. Ultimately, to play is to risk being spontaneous, and perhaps even foolish, which is too scary for the co-dependent. Children in alcoholic families are in a hurry to grow up. Parents of these children often say about them that they are "6 years old going on 40." Being all grown up some day is important, but losing the ability to play is a disaster.

For the person having grown up with this rule, it is very hard to think of ever regaining the childlike ability to play. "Now that you are an adult, you should act like one," we tell ourselves. The child in us wants to play, but we won't let the child out.

Rule 8. Don't rock the boat.

Every family is a system . . . like the organs in the body. Each person in the family has a special part, like actors in a play; and the family rules help each person to know his or her part. Family rules make it easier for us to know what is right, what is wrong, at what age we should be doing certain things, and so on. Stability is one of the positive results of healthy family rules. The rules keep everything in balance, and they let the entire family know when the system is upset . . . just as pain or fever lets your body know that something within its system is upset.

When Timmy gets a negative report from school, or Mom gets a serious illness, the family rules say that something should be done to restore the system to some kind of balance. Mom and Dad talk to Timmy's teacher, or Dad and the kids change their schedules to handle the work that Mom can't do. The system seeks balance. All systems do. Adjusting to change is a healthy quality of systems. In families with unresolved chemical or co-dependency issues, the system also seeks to hold onto a type of balance, but the balance it seeks to maintain is an unhealthy one. The rules it fights so hard to hang onto make it difficult for each person in the system to grow, mature or become healthier. Suzy becomes constantly anxious because Mom and Dad are fighting all the time, but the rules of the system say, "We don't talk about problems," or, "We don't show our sad feelings," so Suzy keeps them inside. Is Suzy doing something wrong, according to the family system? No. Like the actors in the play Suzy is doing her part to keep the system in balance. She's not rocking the boat.

In other words, the system seeks to maintain itself. The flaw in this system is that the family rules do not allow for healthy change. Dad doesn't want to give up drinking because it will be painful to do so. Everyone agrees not to rock the boat because it might make Dad more upset; and if Dad gave up drinking, everyone else in the family might have to change, too, and change can be frightening. However, with enough help and support, the fear of change can be overcome and recovery can take place.

"Don't rock the boat" is the rule which oversees and directs all the other rules in the family. In healthy families, this rule is transformed into, "It's okay to change and grow, your family will always be with you."

The co-dependent individual can be locked inside a set of unhealthy family rules. Until the individual recognizes this trap and challenges these rules; he/she will remain stuck in a co-dependent reality where he/she feels powerless to change. Worst of all is the fact that living inside this trap means that the person can never really let his true feelings show and the private self, the child, remains hidden, isolated and alone. Because this private self is not allowed to come out, real closeness and intimacy with self and others is very hard to achieve. "Am I loved for what I do . . . or am I loved for who I am?"

Putting It All Together

We have said a lot about rules and systems and how they relate to co-dependency and chemical dependency. Basically, the way that we learn to live our lives and interact with others is acquired from our families as we grow up, whether that family be Mom and

Dad, or Dad and Stepmom, or Mom and Grandma. The rules which we have discussed are examples of some of the ways in which families can unconsciously create the conditions for co-dependency or chemical dependency to develop. Why do some people escape the negative consequences? We don't know for sure, but research suggests that they may have formed an attachment to someone who was outside the family system long enough so that they were able to choose healthier ways of living. Perhaps this other person was an aunt or an uncle or the parent of a friend.

Our point is that the rules teach us how to live and solve problems, and that these rules are passed down from one generation to the next, not by heredity or genetics, but by learning . . . by watching and learning. Also the more we live with these rules, the more we practice them in our daily lives; the more we find ourselves exposed to other people who are also co-dependent or chemically dependent, the more we experience living with these rules; then the more we tend to internalize these rules and practice them in our own lives.

Although it may seem controversial, what many professionals are also beginning to realize is that a large number of people who have become chemically dependent were first experiencing the pain of co-dependency. Whether or not they had inherited, through their genes, a tendency toward chemical addiction, many of these people turn to chemicals in an effort to medicate the pain of their already existing co-dependent condition. Many people who have begun the recovery process from chemical dependency are now finding that the next step in achieving greater peace of mind is to begin working on their underlying co-dependencies. What many people call a "dry drunk" in the non using chemically dependent person is, at least in part, the expression of unresolved co-dependencies in his/her life. Ongoing relationship problems, irritability and moodiness are all signs that the person may be operating according to the rules which say, "don't talk," "be perfect," "don't rock the boat," etc. Getting overly involved in one relationship to the exclusion of self, friends and associates is also a sign of unresolved co-dependency. Until we start to live by a new set of rules, the pain will remain.

What Can Be Done?

Does it sound like co-dependency and chemical dependency are such a tangle of rules and dynamics that no one can ever really get away from them? Are we enslaved by our childhoods forever, forced to live by a set of rules which make our lives miserable? No! As is already known, millions of people in this country are now living full happy lives, as a result of various chemical dependency treatment programs: Al-Anon; Alcoholics Anonymous and, most recently, Adult Children of Alcoholic Groups. By the same token, many people are beginning to recognize their co-dependencies, whether or not they had ever lived with a chemically dependent person. Most important is the fact that these co-dependents can also recover and live by new rules. They are learning that they do not have to be afraid of expressing their opinions or showing how they feel. They are learning that they do not have to stay in relationships which cause only misery and grief. And they are learning that life can be peaceful and even fun . . . that the world is not as difficult or dark or lonely as they once had thought. Through established self-help groups like Al-Anon, Alateen, Alatot, Adult Children of Alcoholics, and many new co-dependency treatment programs which are springing up across the country, people are learning that the chain can be broken. The rules can be changed.

While change is almost always risky and scary, in this case the benefits of learning new rules are well worth it: clear sense of self, peace of mind and comfortable relationships.

A Check-Up

Following is a chart which we have found to be helpful in assessing one's progress in coming to terms with co-dependencies. The list is not all-inclusive, but it does serve as a rough guideline. Two or three times per year, try to rate yourself on each item to check your changes. Use a 5-7 or 7-point scale, like the one in this example:

(It's not okay to play.)   1 2 3 4 5   (I let myself have fun.)

Reviewing a chart like this can be especially helpful while you are in the middle of a difficult crisis or conflict. It can serve as a beacon or guide to help you stay on track, or maintain your resolve to change. The most difficult time, of course, is when you are in the middle of a crisis, or in a conflict with someone, and your co-dependencies come into play.

Co-dependency Rules		Growth-Enhancing Rules
1. It's not okay to talk about problems.	1 2 3 4 5	I try to share my problems and get feedback about myself from others.
2. Feelings should not be expressed openly.	1 2 3 4 5	I try to express any persistent feeling with the appropriate person.
3. Communication is indirect, using "messengers."	1 2 3 4 5	I speak for myself directly to whoever is appropriate for the message.
4. Unrealistic expectations.	1 2 3 4 5	I am learning to let go of perfection, details and being "right" all the time.
5. Don't be selfish (guilt).	1 2 3 4 5	Doing things just for me is healthy. I enjoy caring for me.
6. Do as I say, not as I do.	1 2 3 4 5	I try to follow through with actions, not just words.
7. It's not okay to play.	1 2 3 4 5	I let myself have fun. I can even be silly sometimes.

6

Co-dependency: An Emerging Problem

BY

C H A R L E S   L .   W H I T F I E L D

C o-alcoholism can be defined as ill health, or maladaptive or problematic behavior that is associated with living, working with or otherwise being close to a person with alcoholism. It is manifested by a spectrum of symptoms, signs and problems that span from no symptoms at all to headaches to suicide (Table 6.1). It affects not only individuals, but families, communities, businesses and other institutions and states and countries. It has also been called "para" or "near-alcoholism" and "co-dependence." The identification of co-alcoholic patients can be elusive, the diagnosis and confrontation frustrating, the family dynamics complicated and the treatment complex.

Analogous to other chronic illness as alcoholism progresses in one family member, the other members repress their feelings and learn to react with survival behavior. Each member builds a wall of behavioral defenses to cover the painful core of repressed feelings. These "emotional ramparts" follow a common pattern, starting with the alcoholic and the "chief enabler," who is often the spouse, a parent or a child.

At first, the co-alcoholic may see the active alcoholic's inconsistent and inappropriate behavior as either normal (e.g., "Everyone needs to blow off some steam once in a while"), or due to another problem (e.g., "With those job pressures anyone would drink"). Eventually, the alcoholic begins to project his or her pain onto others. As a result these others often feel hurt, self-doubt, shame, inadequacy and guilt. Those who are most distant from the alcoholic frequently react by becoming even more distant, and thus avoiding the alcoholic. However, those who are closer commonly react by accepting the blame, and then attempt to remedy the situation by trying to control the person's drinking and negative behavior. A common pattern while the alcoholic is drinking is that he/she accuses or blames the co-alcoholic, and when he/she is not drinking, the co-alcoholic accuses or blames the alcoholic.

Table 6-1. Examples of Manifestations of Co-alcoholism

In Patients and Clients (Children and Adults)

Behavioral or psychological symptoms such as anxiety, depression, insomnia, hyperactivity, or aggression
Functional or psychosomatic illness
Family violence or neglect
Alcoholism or another chemical dependence of "drug problem"

In the Helping Professional

Failure to make the diagnosis of alcoholism
Failure to treat alcoholism as a primary illness
Treating the alcoholic with long-term sedatives or minor tranquilizers
Treating the co-alcoholic with sedatives or minor tranquilizers

In Society-at-Large

Not confronting relatives, friends and colleagues who are inappropriately intoxicated
Placing a positive social value upon those who drink
Stigmatizing those who are alcoholic or who do not drink

These close people become unwitting enablers of continued drinking out of care, concern, a lack of knowledge and repression of feelings. This enabling is accomplished by the unconscious use of the same defense mechanisms that are active in the alcoholic — denial, repression, rationalization, projection, grandiosity and others. These are defenses used to some degree by everyone. However, their use becomes exaggerated due to the increased stresses and double binds of having to live with an actively drinking alcoholic in an already enabling society.

Unable to ventilate his/her feelings, and unable to see any way out of the predicament, the co-alcoholic often develops one or more of a wide variety of psychological, physical or social illnesses or maladaptive behaviors (Table 6.1). Even the children of alcoholic parents often develop one or more of these problems, which they commonly carry into adulthood. Many co-alcoholic people come from a family of origin in which alcohol has been a problem.

The moderately to severely impaired co-alcoholic person can be viewed as having his/her own addiction. This addiction is in trying to control the alcoholic's drinking behavior, and it is characterized by repeatedly attempting to protect, control and/or change the alcoholic, even though they are usually unsuccessful. Paradoxically, as the alcoholic gradually loses control and power over his drinking and his life, he wields more and more power over those people close to him. There is a gradual loss of individualization by each family member, which is replaced by enmeshment of the family.

One author described seven stages of adjustment to alcoholism: denial, attempts to control the problem, disorganization, substitution, separation, reorganization and reformation. Once the diagnosis of alcoholism or co-alcoholism is made, those afflicted commonly have to repeat these reactions as a normal and healthy part of their recovery.

There are several unwritten rules that tend to become operative in many families where there is alcoholism. These are: (1) The alcoholic's drinking is the most important thing in the family's life; (2) Alcohol is not the cause of the family's problem; (3) Someone or something else caused the alcoholic's dependency; (4) The status quo must be maintained at all costs; (5) Everyone in the family must be an enabler; (6) No one may discuss what is really going on in the family, either with one another or with outsiders (the "family secret"); and (7) No one may say what he/she is really feeling. In most cases, without his/her group of enabling co-alcoholics, the alcoholic would have had to face the consequences of his actions long before his dependency on drinking could have developed into moderately advanced, full-blown alcoholism.

The co-alcoholic's psychopathology, illness and maladaptive behavior are commonly transmitted to others, who may include children, other family members, co-workers and others. Some co-alcoholic patients have been described as being "sicker than their alcoholic". It is not uncommon to see such family members with major psychiatric illness or debilitating physical illness, which is largely secondary to their co-alcoholism.

Like alcoholism, co-alcoholism is a progressive illness. If the alcoholic does not recover, or if the co-alcoholic has no treatment, both illnesses tend to get worse in a parallel fashion. Sometimes, if the alcoholic gets help, but the co-alcoholic does not, the co-alcoholism may remain dormant. Or it may progress, in spite of the alcoholic's recovering. During this progression, the co-alcoholic patient may take on an aggressive or a passive response, or both. An aggressive response may include repulsion, hatred, fantasies and dreams of the alcoholic's death, attempts to hurt the alcoholic, hatred of sex, attempts to avoid communication, verbal and physical abuse and temporary separation or desertion. A passive response may include hiding feelings, withdrawal, extended crying, obsession with cleanliness or work, bargaining prayers, and giving all love and attention to the children, phobias, anxiety disorders, and developing symptoms which may get the alcoholic's or other's attention. However, these responses are nearly always ineffective, and tend to promote further progression of the co-alcoholism.

Similar ineffective aggressive and passive behavior is commonly seen among others close to alcoholics including friends, co-workers, supervisors, administrators, helping professionals, law enforcement workers and politicians. It may be that co-alcoholic men take on a more aggressive response and that women take on a more passive response. As an example, men tend to leave their alcoholic wives sooner than women tend to leave their alcoholic husbands.

Making the Diagnosis

When a patient presents any of the manifestations listed in Table 6-1, it is helpful to ask, "Have you ever been concerned about the drinking (or drug use) of anyone close to you?" If the answer is yes, or if the patient is vague or doubtful, one can administer the Family Drinking Survey (end of article). One can also ask the prospective co-alcoholic to answer the questions truthfully on the Michigan Alcoholism Screening Test as though the questions are addressed to the potentially-alcoholic person to whom he or she is close. A positive score on either test is a strong indication of co-alcoholism.

The following are some clinical clues suggested by Wegscheider. When the patient manifests any of the following, consider co-alcoholism.

1. *Super-responsibility:* "If I don't take care of things, they just won't get done."
2. *Pseudo-fragility:* "I don't know how much more of this I can take!"
3. *Hypochondria:* "I hardly get over one cold when I catch another."
4. *Powerlessness:* "I've tried everything to get him to stop."
5. *Self-blame:* "I should have planned for that."

These are all defensive postures by which a co-alcoholic avoids looking honestly at his/her position and doing something about it. This is not to say that every hypochondriac, for example, is married to or is the child of an alcoholic. But where several of these symptoms are present, alcoholism in the family, and thus co-alcoholism, should be suspected.

Any alcoholic's family member, other close person, friend, co-worker, or even a more distant person may become a co-alcoholic. Anyone living with or close to an active alcoholic who is not satisfactorily recovering in Al-Anon or by some other treatment can be presumed to be co-alcoholic. For those whose close person is dependent upon a drug other than alcohol, the term co-chemical dependent can be used. While co-alcoholism should be considered in the differential diagnosis of the complaints in Table 6.1, other possible etiologies should be ruled out in an appropriate fashion. A patient can also have a dual or multiple diagnosis of co-alcoholism and one or more other conditions, including alcoholism.

Even if the alcoholic stops drinking, there is a need for the co-alcoholic to get treatment. Otherwise, the co-alcoholic continues to try to control, becomes ill, or becomes a scapegoat.

The Role of the Helping Professional

Underlying and feeding the vicious cycles of alcoholism and co-alcoholism are ignorance and denial on the part of the victims and the rest of society. Until these factors can be corrected, it is likely that alcoholism and co-alcoholism will remain a pervasive problem in this country and in the world. It is estimated that there are about 10 million alcoholics in the U.S., and that for every alcoholic there are from three to five people seriously affected by being around the alcoholic, or between 30 and 50 million co-alcoholics. Some alcoholics are in the same families, and thus these figures might be lower for co-alcoholics.

These 30 to 50 million people often develop symptoms severe enough to seek help. Unfortunately, many helping professionals are not trained to recognize, manage or refer these patients appropriately. The helper often treats the symptom without addressing the co-alcoholism itself. For example, the physican may prescribe a sedative-hypnotic, minor tranquilizer or anti-depressant drug without carefully evaluating the person's life situation. Or he/she may launch into an extensive (and expensive) medical or psychological work-up. Or the psychotherapist may treat the psychological symptom or sign with intensive psychotherapy or behavior therapy. Or the social worker, lawyer, clergy or other helping professional may address the more external problems, and not the co-alcoholism. By doing so, the helper is unknowingly acting as an enabler of continued co-alcoholism. Most helping professionals are not adequately taught in their professional schools about alcoholism, the enabling process or their treatment. These can be called the "untrained" or "untreated professional".

The Untreated Professional

A concept in the field of chemical dependency which has gained recognition is that of the untreated professional; defined as a helping professional, supervisor or administrator who is also a co-alcoholic, and who has not had treatment specifically for the co-alcoholism. The dynamics are the same as those for all co-alcoholics. However, a major difference is that the untreated professional can spread the illness of co-alcoholism to many more people and can, under the guise of "helping," actually harm them.

Since nearly all untreated or untrained people in the general population are to some degree co-alcoholic, even though they are not now, or have not been in the past, closely related to or associated with an alcoholic, a common and important variation on the untreated professional enters the picture: the professional who has not been trained in the modern skills of alcoholism/chemical dependency recognition and treatment, or the "Untrained Professional." I estimate that today, conservatively, 80% of all helping professionals remain untrained in this crucial area. A major reason for this fact is that the faculty and administrators of their professional schools are themselves untrained and/or untreated professionals. This disease of co-alcoholism deceives them into thinking and saying that they are teaching what "needs" to be taught about alcoholism/chemical dependency. Thus, they continue spreading their own lack of knowledge and skills to the many thousands of their students, who then go out and deliver incomplete or inadequate help to their patients and clients . . . and the vicious cycle continues.

Another term for the untrained or untreated professional is the "Professional Enabler," whom Wegscheider further describes as "any helping professional who engages in the same kinds of dysfunctional behavior as the family Enabler — denial, avoidance, covering up, protecting, taking responsibility for someone else, either the Dependent or another family member . . . He may not realize that helping in the normal sense of the word — that is, trying to fix things — is not helpful in this situation. It will only prolong the problem."

The Institutionalization of an Illness

Co-alcoholism commonly occurs among people working in institutions, the media, politics and elsewhere. If alcoholism and co-alcoholism are unchecked, they breed negativity for everyone they touch, and we need to know how to handle them. The following is an example illustrating such a problem area:

A medical school associate dean was blocking the delivery of teaching about alcoholism as a disease, including the production of teaching materials. He did this for about two years, causing much difficulty for the two faculty members

who were teaching the material. When asked why he blocked
the teaching, he would reply that it was because the teachers
were not following the rules of the medical school. The other
deans and administrative staff supported him. It was later
discovered that he was an active alcoholic. Most of his peers
knew he was a heavy drinker, but they denied he might have
an alcohol problem and that it was affecting his work, and
they would not push him into treatment.

How could the two teachers deal with this resistance? Consideration must be given to the fact that they were junior faculty members dealing with an administrative hierarchy. A major reason why the VIP alcoholic can be so difficult to handle and treat is that he has such powerful enablers. One possible solution, if their state had an impaired physician program, would be to refer him to the medical society's rehabilitation committee. If such a program were effective, this would be the most direct and positive way to handle such a common situation and a disabled colleague. Even under such circumstances, rehabilitation may take from one to five years, during which time he may be ·recovering successfully enough to change his attitude and stop blocking the teachers' attempts at progress. Data suggest that 10% of faculty and administration are active alcoholic or chemically dependent. The co-alcoholics could be suggested to attend Al-Anon, although such VIP's are often the most resistant to such a suggestion.

There are numerous other examples of co-alcoholism among institutions and within political systems. Seven of these follow:

1. Hospitals refusing to treat alcoholics for their alcoholism, while treating them for the medical and psychological consequences of their alcoholism.
2. Health insurance carriers excluding alcoholism treatment from standard coverage; treatment is covered only with an extra cost alcoholism rider, and here payment is made only for expensive inpatient, and not for less expensive outpatient or residential treatment.
3. The criminal justice system spending more money on incarceration and processing of alcohol-related crimes, while not developing liaisons with local alcoholism treatment programs which would probably be the most effective deterrent to criminal recidivism.

4. A legal and judicial system neither diverting drunk drivers who are alcoholic into treatment, nor prosecuting them.
5. Schools suspending or expelling students for alcohol-related offenses instead of seeing that they get appropriate treatment.
6. A state government collecting 100 million dollars in liquor taxes and allocating 10 million dollars as its total effort in alcoholism treatment.
7. The Federal Communications Commission's disallowing distilled alcoholic beverages to be advertised on television, but not wine and beer.

A common trend through these examples is the denial that alcoholism is causal of each problem area and denial that alcoholism is a primary and treatable illness.

Role	Motivating Feeling	Indentifying Symptoms	Payoff		Possible Price
			Individual	Family	
Dependent	Shame	Chemical use	Relief of pain	None	Addiction
Enabler	Anger	Powerlessness	Importance; self-right-eousness	Responsibility	Illness; "martyrdom"
Hero	Inadequacy; guilt	Overachieve-ment	Attention (positive)	Self-worth	Compulsive drive
Scapegoat	Hurt	Delinquency	Attention (negative)	Focus away from depen-dent	Self-destruc-tion; addiction
Lost Child	Loneliness	Solitariness; shyness	Escape	Relief	Social isolation
Mascot	Fear	Clowning; hyperactivity	Attention (amused)	Fun	Immaturity; emotional illness
Untreated/ untrained Professional	Desire to help	Unsuccessful treatment	Temporary symptom relief	Temporary relief	Treatment failure; burn-out

Conclusion

Co-alcoholism is a newly-recognized, treatable diagnostic entity. Initially, it is a normal response to an abnormal situation. However, it may often lead the individual to become dysfunctional. It is chronic, progressive and characterized by denial, ill health or maladaptive behavior, and by a lack of knowledge about alcoholism. While there is little in the literature about it, there appears to be a rational and effective approach to its diagnosis and treatment. The condition needs further research.

Co-alcoholism and co-chemical dependence are more prevalent problems than the number of primary addictions. Focusing on this segment, which includes, in addition to family members, most helping professionals, law enforcement workers, politicians, employers and others, could result in a cultural change that would force the alcoholic or other chemical dependent into treatment much sooner. In other words, education of this group could stop the enabling, cover-up and the seductive diversion into other treatments, or the promoting of drugs with abuse and dependence potential.

FAMILY DRINKING SURVEY

1. Does someone in your family undergo personality changes when he or she drinks to excess?
2. Do you feel that drinking is more important to this person than you are?
3. Do you feel sorry for yourself and frequently indulge in self-pity because of what you feel alcohol is doing to your family?
4. Has some family member's excessive drinking ruined special occasions?
5. Do you find yourself covering up for the consequences of someone else's drinking?
6. Have you ever felt guilty, apologetic, or responsible for the drinking of a member of your family?
7. Does one of your family member's use of alcohol cause fights and arguments?
8. Have you ever tried to fight the drinker by joining in the drinking?
9. Do the drinking habits of some family members make you feel depressed or angry?
10. Is your family having financial difficulties because of drinking?
11. Did you ever feel like you had an unhappy home life because of the drinking of some members of your family?
12. Have you ever tried to control the drinker's behavior by hiding the car keys, pouring liquor down the drain, etc.?
13. Do you find yourself distracted from your responsibilities because of this person's drinking?

14. Do you often worry about a family member's drinking?
15. Are holidays more of a nightmare than a celebration because of a family member's drinking behavior?
16. Are most of your drinking family member's friends heavy drinkers?
17. Do you find it necessary to lie to employers, relatives or friends in order to hide your spouse's drinking?
18. Do you find yourself responding differently to members of your family when they are using alcohol?
19. Have you ever been embarrassed or felt the need to apologize for the drinker's actions?
20. Does some family member's use of alcohol make you fear for your own safety or the safety of other members of your family?
21. Have you ever thought that one of your family members had a drinking problem?
22. Have you ever lost sleep because of a family member's drinking?
23. Have you ever encouraged one of your family members to stop or cut down on their drinking?
24. Have you ever threatened to leave home or to leave family members because of their drinking?
25. Did a family member ever make promises that he or she did not keep because of their drinking.
26. Have you ever felt sick, cried, or had a "knot" in your stomach after worrying about a family member's drinking?
27. Has a family member ever failed to remember what occurred during a drinking period?
28. Does your family member avoid social situations where alcoholic beverages would not be served?
29. Does your family member have periods of remorse after drinking occasions and apologize for his or her behavior?

7

Co-dependency As The Invader Of Intimacy

BY

J A N E T   G E R I N G E R   W O I T I T Z

Where did it go wrong? What happened? Who is responsible? Where is the sense? What does it all mean? Where will it all end? Circles and circles of circle and circles — all filled with confusion. Where did we go off the track? Is it possible to understand?

For each couple the beginning is different. Even so, the process that occurs in the chemically dependent marital relationship is essentially the same. For the starting point, let's take a look at the marriage vows. Most wedding services include the following statements — for better or worse — for richer or poorer — in sickness and in health — until death do us part. Maybe that's where all the trouble began. Did you mean what you said when you said it? If you knew at that time that you were going to have not the better but the worse, not the health but the sickness, not the richer but the poorer, and the potential suicide, would the love that you felt have made it worth it? You may say so, but I wonder. If you were more realistic than romantic, you may have interpreted the vows to mean — through the bad as well as the good, assuming that the bad times would be transitory and the good ones permanent. The contract is entered into in good faith. There is no benefit of hindsight.

The idealizing that takes place at this time is not realistic. This is true not only for those who will live with chemical dependence, but for everyone. The difference is that the reality continues to be distorted in the chemically dependent relationship, and little by little the couple loses touch with what a happy marital relationship is all about. If the statistics are accurate, and they probably are understated, then a very large percentage of you grew up in chemically dependent households. This is important to be aware of because you probably had no idea how to develop a healthy marital relationship to begin with. Your early attempts to "do it right" were built on models that you had not seen or experienced, but rather made up in your own head. Thus, the fancifulness of the vows would play right into this notion of "It will be different for us."

By the time help is sought, the expectations have changed a great deal. The sense of self is gone for the chemically free partner. "How can I help him/her?" The sense of what one can expect in a relationship has shifted. It is no longer Camelot. It is no longer even person to person. The distortion is bizarre. I will stay because . . . "He doesn't beat me." "She doesn't run around." "He hasn't lost his job." Imagine getting credit for the behaviors we ordinary mortals do as a matter of course. Even if the worst is true. Even if he does beat you. Even if she does run around. Even if he is no longer working. Even with all this, you will then say, "But I love him/her!" When I respond, "Tell me, what is so lovable?" there is no response. The answer doesn't come, but the power of being emotionally stuck is far greater than the power of reason.

Somewhere between the vows of everlasting wonderfulness and the acceptance of life as a horror story lies the reality. Somewhere hidden in the muck is the truth. It didn't get distorted overnight. It started out on one end of the pendulum and landed on the other.

Somehow the process was so gradual that no one saw it happening and the middle ground went unnoticed.

If I ask, "What was lovable when you decided to marry?" the response comes quickly. It is not unusual to hear answers like, "There was a strong physical attraction and we could talk about anything and everything. He/she was my lover and my best friend."

These sentiments are sincere and important. It is important to recognize that people who start out as friends and lovers have something special . . . It is important, therefore, to recognize that chemical dependency affects everything. It turns lovers and friends into adversaries. Friendship is based on a number of things. It is based on mutual trust and honesty. It is based on the ability to communicate openly. It is based on a sense of understanding and being understood. The chemical dependency eats away at these, slowly but surely.

The erosion probably begins in the denial phase. At this stage, the drinking is causing problems but no one wants to face up to it. So the lies begin. First the lies to self, and then the lies to each other. The dependent person will lie mostly in terms of broken promises. The chemically free person will lie to cover up. The trust begins to break down. True feelings are held back until they become explosive. The honest communication begins to dissolve.

The physical relationship is a good indicator of what is happening in the total relationship. The attraction may well continue through the denial phase. It will continue to be a way of sharing, even as the words become more difficult. Not only that, but no one has yet to come up with a better way of making up after a drunken episode.

Gradually, the interest in physical intimacy will decline on the part of the chemically free partner. The need to be less vulnerable will start to take over. At this point the sexual experience may still be technically satisfying, but the emotion is held in check.

As in all other aspects, the deterioration continues and what was a warm, loving experience now becomes a power play and a means of ventilating anger.

"Go to bed with your bottle — not me!" "I can't stand the smell!" "You have to make a choice!" "Who needs you! It won't be hard to find someone better than you!"

The gap continues to get greater. No part of the relationship remains unaffected.

The climate becomes confused and the open communication that existed before gives way to suspicion and anger. The underlying concerns are not addressed and the couple, even though they still care about each other, live a distorted lifestyle. Both partners are being directed by the chemical — one directly, the other indirectly. One is addicted to the chemical — the other is addicted to the chemically dependent partner.

The relationship breaks down even further . . . If the chemical dependency was only destructive to this point, the damage to the relationship is repairable. It is possible to argue it out and at the very least, clear the air. Feelings can be expressed and the lines of communication can remain open. But this is not simple.

The insidious illness does not stop here. It separates the couple still further. The chemically dependent partner stops developing emotionally. The chemically dependent partner no longer wants to deal with or confront problems. A large part of any marital relationship is making decisions and resolving shared problems. Where will we go on our vacation? Johnny is failing algebra again. Can we redo the kitchen?

And so on with the stuff that life is made of. These issues are no longer shared. The chemically free partner takes over more and more responsibility. The resentment grows deeper. The gap becomes even greater.

A saving grace during difficult times is the support of caring family and friends. This is true here, too, at least for a while, but if they have not experienced what you are experiencing, the support will only increase the pain. If they could only understand. The isolation of the chemically dependent couple becomes greater. They become isolated from other people and they move further and further away from each other.

And the sickness continues. The feelings shared are similar. The pain and the desperation are felt by both, but they blame each other. The guilt is felt by both but the responsibility is placed differently. Once close, you are now strangers most of the time.

Occasionally, you will find yourselves in the eye of the storm and you will be so grateful. The idea is that now the drinking will stop and all will be as it was. It is a shared belief. It is a shared deception. The reality is that the disease will progress. It will get worse . . . and so will whatever is left of your relationship.

The communication deteriorates into forms of anger. The inner feelings evolve into worry, fear and despair. The feelings are shared, but in isolation. The chemically dependent partner numbs the feelings and the non-abuser is doubled over in pain — relieved only by anger and occasional fantasies.

The fantasy is that the drinking will stop and everything w\
as it was in the beginning. The miracle of abstinence. The fan\
is shared. Alcohol will lose its hold and you will live happily ever
after.

Somehow that is the greatest lie of all, and yet one of the most
universally believed. The drinking stops. What does that mean in
terms of the relationship? It only means that the focus is lost. It only
means that the chemical is no longer the focal point. A huge
vacuum now exists. Nothing else happens automatically. The trust
that was lost does not come back just because the abuse stops. Just
as a history of unfulfilled promises damaged the trust, a new history
has to come into play in order to rebuild it. The lies may stop, but
sharing makes one too vulnerable to be open at this point. The
anger does not automatically go away because the drinking stops.
The feelings that were repressed by the chemical may want to
come cascading out. How terribly insecure — how terribly
frightened. How hard to share these feelings and expect to be
understood. The lines of communication have been cut off. You are
two blind people without a road map.

Abstinence is not enough. A whole new relationship has to be
built. The new starting point has to be different from the original
starting point. The starting point this time is best served in learning
how to solve mutual problems. It is best served in developing
guidelines of how to talk to and not at each other. How can each
be heard and understood? If the relationship is going to be healthy,
it is going to require a lot of hard work. The foundation will require
careful and long attention. The attraction that enhances the
beginning of a relationship is no longer present. The basis now has
to be firmly grounded in reality. If both parties are committed to
working, it can be more than it would have been, had the chemical
not entered the picture. If both people are looking for the same
things, there is a great opportunity for mutual, as well as individual
growth. If not, the fantasy is over. The relationship is done.
Abstinence is not nirvana.

Chemical dependency destroys slowly, but thoroughly. Chemical
independency can lead the way to build a healthy marital
relationship. It's the only winning game in town.

8

Sexuality Issues During Recovery

BY

M A R I L Y N M A S O N

F
ear of intimacy is often based on fear of sexuality. Since fear of intimacy is a primary issue in recovery, it is only natural that sexuality is also problematic in recovery. Indeed, many sexual health professionals report that more than half of their clients are in chemically dependent relationships. Conversely, at least half of the people who seek chemical dependency treatment have sexual concerns.

In order to present the argument that recovery must be based on a redefinition of sexuality, including its spiritual dimension, we must begin with specific definitions. To those, we must add the assumptions underlying the clinical concerns before moving toward the spiritual dimension.

Definitions

In any discussion of sexuality in recovery, two definitions are relevant:

Sexuality is, in the broadest sense, the human/psychic energy that finds physical and emotional expression in the desire for contact, warmth, tenderness and love.

Chemical dependency is the spiritual dis-ease involving the denial of intimacy. This dependent state results from addiction to chemicals, such as alcohol, amphetamines, or hallucinogens.

If we can agree on both definitions, we can gain a clearer understanding of the inter-relatedness and significance of sexuality and chemical dependency to intimacy in a healthy recovery.

Assumption One. No-talk rules govern both sexuality and chemical dependency. The conspiracy of silence and the lack of comfortable language result in the rhetoric of avoidance. It is only natural that professionals who have not been able to break their own no-talk rules will bring them into their work settings. The following example clearly bears this out: During an in-house workshop on sexuality, a treatment center chaplain stated, "Why, I've heard 2000 Fifth Steps, and I've never heard a sexual concern yet!" On the third morning of the workshop, he rushed in and exclaimed, "I don't know what happened, but I heard three sexual concerns last night!" Having broken his own no-talk rule, he was, for the first time, able to give his clients permission to break theirs.

Assumption Two. Intimacy is not a steady or fixed state; it is a life-long search, beginning and ending with dependent states. From developmental psychology, we understand that adolescence is the time when intimacy in paired relationships becomes established. It is not surprising, then, that people in recovery often say that they feel like teenagers. This is quite accurate, considering it was during adolescence when many of them shut down, numbing themselves with chemicals to ease their fear of sexual feelings and to give themselves permission to be sexual.

Assumption Three. People can be stripped of their chemicals, but will always be sexual. Many people learned to be sexual by lowering their inhibitions with alcohol or other drugs. When they attempt closeness without relying on chemicals, they often find the experience to be terrifying.

Assumption Four. Our love relationships have been based on the pathological model that two persons who pair will become one. Because this model does not allow for separateness in relationships, it has fostered dependency. Therefore, treatment centers face a real challenge in presenting the natural model of today. You will have to do battle with the age-old urge-to-merge feeling of fusion (that catharsis called "love").

Assumption Five. Sexuality has long been viewed as an outcome, rather than a process. In our product-oriented, shame-based society, we often quantify sexual behaviors and equate quantity to quality. In short, we have focused on genitality, not sexuality. As a result, individuals have learned how to come together, but most long to learn how to come together. In process-oriented sex, the focus is on the "together" aspect, and for many this causes a greater fear than the more "genital" approach with non-person sex (sex with nobody home). Sexual competence is indeed helpful, but does not bring love into loving. Songwriter Michael Johnson titled a song: *Love Will Get You Through Times Of No Sex Better Than Sex Will Get You Through Times Of No Love.*

Assumption Six. A sexual recovery is only as full as the spiritual recovery. Theologian Henri Nouwen states in *Reaching Out* that the first stage of spiritual growth is establishing a relationship with the self. Since this is also the first stage of the recovery process, one's sexual acceptance will be primary in recovery.

Sexual Concerns in Treatment

The sexual concerns most frequently held by clients in treatment are: extra-marital sex, anorgasmia, erectile dysfunction, gay/lesbian relationships, incest, and sexual addiction. Of course, these same concerns exist in the general population, but their frequency and intensity are greater in the chemically dependent.

Extramarital sex is often a guilt-ridden issue in treatment and recovery. Many individuals become involved outside their paired relationship or marriage while using chemicals. Many have struggled with their attempts to disprove their dependency or end a relationship by having an affair. Neither partner realizes at the time that he/she is in collusion with the other; extra-marital sex is always at least a two-person affair. One partner does not walk out

the door unless the other is knowingly or unknowingly holding it
at least partially open. The residual guilt and resentments
associated with extra-marital sex place great stress on individuals as
well as couples in recovery. The guilt and remorse, which may not
be disclosed during the early stages of treatment, must be worked
through in the recovery process.

Anorgasmia (formerly called frigidity) is frequently reported by
both recovering women and Al-Anon wives. Sexual guilt and a fear
of lack of control have been observed in many recovering women.
Both can result in anorgasmia. Many recovering women who are
struggling with boundary concerns fear that they might become too
loose, become objects, if they allow themselves to be orgasmic, yet
they do not want to fake orgasms. Another contributing factor in
anorgasmia is a history of forced intercourse. Repressed or active
anger is most often anorgasmia's closest friend. Orgasms require a
total loss of control; it is difficult for a woman to let go of this
control until she knows she has some control. Fear and lack of trust
have caused many women to become almost asexual. While
women can be encouraged to discover their sexual values, the art
of self-pleasuring or masturbation seems to be the number one
factor in helping these women achieve orgasms.

Erectile Dysfunction (formerly called impotence) is common
among men in recovery. In fact, erectile functioning may not return
to normal for up to 12 weeks following treatment. Drugs affect the
chemical balance in the blood; it takes time for the body's chemical
balance (including the hormone androgen) to return to its normal
level in the blood with abstinence of drugs. Erectile dysfunction is
usually secondary, that is, it is situational and can be relieved.
Alcohol is not the only drug associated with a high incidence of
impotence; one study showed that 50% of heroin addicts had
erectile dysfunction. Men who are discouraged about their sexual
competence often resume drinking because of their emotional
pain regarding their masculinity. In addition, many Al-Anon wives
report feeling sexually inferior and inadequate as women because
they still believe at some level they are responsible for their
husbands' erections. When anorgasmia meets erectile dysfunction,
it is not unusual for couples to refrain from genital sex for 10 to 12
years following treatment.

Gay-Lesbian relationships are now receiving the respect they
long needed in many treatment centers. Some studies show two or
three of every four gays are chemically dependent. Unless gays and
lesbians are allowed to talk openly about their sexual preference,

they will continue to confront the same issues they had prior to treatment or involvement in A.A. If human dignity is the focus of recovery (as indeed it should be), then it is only natural that all non-exploitive loving relationships be respected.

Many heterosexual individuals fear their same-sex fantasies, thinking this means they are gay. Often, all it means is that they have a broad-base for sexual love fantasies. Perhaps what is most needed in treatment is the acknowledgment that we live with the myth that the world is heterosexual. When some individuals are denied the right to express sexual preference, they are also denied the right to recovery with integrity and self-respect.

Incest has been a concern of increasing interest, often with staggeringly high incidences of incest reported in treatment centers. Chemical dependency is present in as many as 50% of incestuous families. Some halfway houses have reported that up to 85% of their female clients are incest victims. If we work in the field of chemical dependency, we will be working with incest, both denied and presented. Counselors in many centers feel overwhelmed by all the sexual abuse issues they encounter. Although they have the obligation to allow these issues to surface, they cannot be expected to treat sexual abuse. The whole family needs incest treatment. Treatment centers can ease their work by working with community agencies for referrals and reporting laws. While many counselors state they feel discomfort in violating their clients' confidentiality in treatment, they surely don't want to contribute to this crime by remaining silent.

Many incest victims avoid A.A. and/or Al-Anon because they fear being touched. When an incest victim is hugged, he/she often freezes in shame and cannot speak out. Clinicians, too, must remember that our need to nurture can be another person's moment of terror.

Of course, not all incest victims are female. Many males have not recognized their victimization; with increased reporting, many more male victims are getting long-needed help.

Sexual addiction is still being discovered in many parts of the country and is increasing in dual-dependency treatment. Many clients in treatment centers and A.A. members have been covering the pain of their primary addiction, sexual addiction with drugs. While the recovery for drug dependence works well for them, they are unable to have serenity because of the remorse and shame brought on by their compulsive sexual behavior (masturbation, heterosexual and gay affairs, marital rape or forced intercourse).

Many members of Sex Addicts Anonymous (12-Step Program) are men, while many women, socialized to have identity through relationships, have joinied Co-SA groups. The number of women who identify themselves as sexual addicts is also increasing.

To be sure, all of these sexual concerns exist in all of society. However, when we talk about them in the context of chemical dependency, we are usually talking about intensification of the behavior — both feelings and frequency. The fear of closeness, which is so natural to the human condition, is therefore intensified in the recovering addict's life.

In recovery, it is important for professionals to recognize that many of these concerns can be greatly alleviated by talking about them. Talking about a sexual concern in an A.A. group or a treatment group can indeed be a risk, but not talking is also a risk. In working with recovering alcoholics, many sex therapists and family therapists have found that greater progress can be made because these people know their feelings, the dimension so basic to a good sexual relationship.

Spirituality and Sexuality

One philosopher has stated: "To be authentically naked in the 20th century is as difficult as being born again." The rebirth-through-recovery will necessitate a discovery of the self through the uncovering of the masks which we have hidden behind, and the facing of our vulnerabilities. Before seeking physical sexual comfort, we will have to face our sexual shame and begin the process of sexual acceptance. Often Fourth and Fifth Step work, specifically related to sexual concerns, is helpful. Journaling of feelings and attitude changes is also helpful. If a whole-person recovery is the goal, then it is important to recognize that the sexual embodiment through integrating our intellectual, emotional and physical selves is primary. This can be the beginning of the spiritual dimension of sexuality.

The intimacy journey can be exciting. When a recovering person can set limits and establish boundaries, then a clear identity is known to him or her as well as to others. And when these two whole separate selves meet one another, they can enjoy intimacy in a variety of areas, including loving and being loved in sexual harmony.

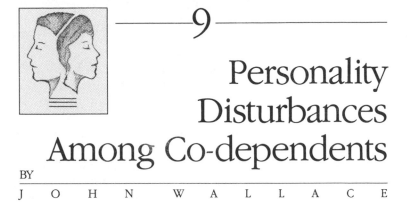

9

Personality Disturbances Among Co-dependents

BY

J O H N   W A L L A C E

M uch of the dysfunctional behavior of family members is stress-related and, hence, an outcome of living near active alcoholism. However, the clinician must not assume that all dysfunctional behavior in the family is situationally determined by the partner's alcoholism. In some cases, personality disturbances in family members exist prior to the onset of alcoholism in a member. In other cases, these may develop independently of it. Obviously, not every problem with a family member can be traced directly to a member's alcoholism. Alcoholism certainly cannot be thought of as protecting family members from the personality disturbances of all kinds that afflict members of families in which alcoholism is not present.

71

There is an obvious danger in construing all family problems as linked in some manner or another to a member's alcoholism. There is the danger that serious psychological problems in family members will be left untreated or treated inappropriately in programs devoted to alcoholism therapy per se. If left untreated, such problems may not only perpetuate suffering in the non-alcoholic member, but complicate the alcoholic's recovery in several ways.

First, a spouse with neurotic problems of his/her own can introduce high levels of stress into a marriage. It can be just as difficult to live near or with a chronic hypochondriac with endless complaints, a phobic personality who refuses to leave the house, or a needy, excessively dependent, possessive, and demanding partner as it is to live with alcoholism. For obvious reasons, such pre-existing neurotic patterns in spouses may make it exceedingly difficult for particular alcoholics to maintain sobriety or to achieve a happy, contented sobriety.

Secondly, in some, but certainly not all spouses, the level and nature of a personality disturbance may be such as to create a need for the partner's alcoholism. Either consciously or unconsciously, these particular spouses with an investment in their partner's alcoholism may interfere with or sabotage the partner's attempt to recover. That this can and does occur in particular marriages cannot be denied, but the generality of such motives is open to question. In particular families with whom I have worked, the sabotage and interference were quite overt and unmistakable. In one case, a young husband repeatedly informed his wife that as far as he was concerned, he would rather have her drinking than sober. His favorite jibe was, "Why don't you go upstairs and suck on your bottle like you used to?" Another husband consistently arranged to meet his alcoholic wife in a bar where he drank and joked with his friends while berating her for ordering soft drinks for herself. A non-alcoholic wife came home with six bottles of rum which she had purchased in the first few months of her husband's sobriety. When questioned by her husband as to why she had done so, the wife explained, "Well, it was on sale and seemed like such a good deal!"

Several groups of wives of alcoholics were identified from examination of MMPI profiles. A high psychopathic deviate score and a typical 4-3-9 profile (psychopathic deviate, hysteria, and hypomania) suggested a type of wife with a high level of psychiatric disturbance who used her husband's alcoholism as a "neurotic defense". The possibility that at least some wives may derive neurotic need satisfaction from a husband's alcoholism is consistent with data reported. In a sample of 116 middle class families, 52% of the wives had married men at a time when the alcoholism problems were already serious. But, of course, there are numerous reasons why a person will knowingly choose an alcoholic mate other than the need to be married to an alcoholic. People often marry alcoholics out of the innocent misconception that marriage to a good man or woman is all alcoholics need, that love alone will straighten them out. Moreover, there are other studies that suggest the opposite of these findings and indicate that spouses are unaware of their mate's alcoholism at the time of their marriage.

Clinical observations of psychological "decompensation" in some spouses after the alcoholic has stopped drinking are consistent with, but not a necessary piece of proof, for the belief that some wives or husbands derive neurotic need satisfaction from their partner's alcoholism. According to the decompensation hypothesis, when the neurotic need satisfaction of the spouse is blocked by the partner's abstinence, the spouse's psychological condition worsens and may become serious enough to require psychiatric hospitalization.

The decompensation hypothesis, like many things in alcoholism theory, is highly controversial. If such breakdowns do occur, they do so at an extremely low rate. Rae (1972), for example, noted that only 4 out of 58 spouses studied had to be hospitalized for psychiatric reasons after the husband achieved abstinence. Jackson (1962), found only one wife in eight years of study who showed an increase in psychological disturbance after her husband achieved sobriety. Other investigators have found that improvements in psychological functioning can be expected in spouses when the alcoholic's drinking ceases. But, of course, the fate of the hypothesis is that some spouses may derive neurotic need satisfaction from marriage to an alcoholic does not hinge upon the fate of the decompensation hypothesis. Spouses with such needs may satisfy them in alternative ways, i.e., deceptive, extra-marital affairs with drinking alcoholics, divorce and remarriage to a drinking alcoholic, realization that such need satisfaction can still occur with an abstinent husband, but in a different form, etc.

In general, then, the evidence concerning possible decompensa tion in the spouse when abstinence is achieved suggests that if it occurs at all, it is not a general phenomenon. Even in the small numbers of cases where it would appear decompensation has occurred, numerous plausible rival explanations are available to explain such breakdowns.

One can conclude that spouses of alcoholics may show reactive, stress-related behavioral dysfunctions, chronic personality disturbances that may have existed prior to marriage to an alcoholic, or behavioral dysfunctions that are a combination of the two — stress interacting with personality disturbance. While all three types of behavioral dysfunctions in spouses can contribute to the maintenance of alcoholism in the family, one cannot conclude that they all derive from a single motivational basis, i.e., the need or desire to prevent recovery and stay married to an active alcoholic. Even when personality disturbances in the spouse exist independently of the partner's alcoholism and impact negatively upon recovery, one must not conclude that the spouse has a neurotic need to maintain the partner's alcoholism. The spouse's contribution to the partner's alcoholism may be unwitting and inadvertent. Personality disturbances in the spouse may simply raise the stress level in the family further and make it difficult for the recovering alcoholic to achieve need satisfactions of his/her own when drunk or sober.

Some unknown numbers of spouses may seek, either overtly or covertly, to maintain their partner's alcoholism for reasons of neurotic need satisfaction. Even in these cases, it is doubtful that the motivational picture is so simplistic and undimensional. Just as the alcoholic presents for treatment in motivational conflict — wanting to stay sober, but wanting to drink — it is likely that some spouses experience a similar conflict of motives.

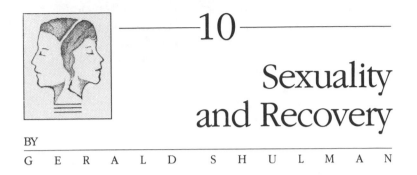

—10—

Sexuality and Recovery

BY

G   E   R   A   L   D   S   H   U   L   M   A   N

I t would be impossible to talk about the role of sexuality in recovery without relating it to the role of sexuality during the active chemical dependence, which impacts on both the chemically dependent person and family member (partner). The focus of this article will primarily be on alcohol, and other sedative/hypnotic drugs, because the scope is not sufficient to allow for a broader discussion of other drugs.

When looking at the impact of sexuality in recovery, major areas that need to be noted are sexual dysfunction, performance anxiety, self-image, past sexual behavior, communication, trust and intimacy. These individual areas are not discrete and may have a cumulative effect on current sexual adjustment and comfort. In this context, recovery is defined as total abstinence and an enhancement of functioning in every major area of a person's life (e.g., work, family, marriage, health, etc.), including self-image.

It is clearly documented that during active dependence, sexual dysfunction is most commonly a direct result of the depressant effects of the sedative/hypnotic drugs. However, during early recovery, chemically dependent people may be surprised by a continuation of the dysfunction because they may assume that the dysfunction is simply a result of being intoxicated. One common example is continued erectile difficulty in newly-recovering males, because of a low testosterone level, which does not immediately rectify itself with sobriety. In both chemically dependent people and their partners, the history of past "failure" and the anxiety about performance may well be the major stumbling block to a relaxed and satisfying sexual relationship, if not a functional one.

In early recovery (less than six months), the recollection of dysfunction problems during the period of active dependence may well negatively affect current ability and interest in sex. The great emphasis placed on sexual performance in this culture, and its subsequent anxiety is further compounded with a recovering chemically dependent/co-dependent person because of the history of dysfunction. The very anxiety about current functioning and the resultant "spectatoring" may become the major obstacle to effective functioning.

The self-image of both the chemically dependent person and partner almost always suffers during active addiction. In addition to the assault on one's value system that is a function of chemical dependence/co-dependence itself, some chemically dependent people and/or their partners may have engaged in sexual (e.g., extra-marital affairs, homosexual behavior, etc.), or no-sexual behaviors (e.g., lying, verbal and physical abuse), which they now find unacceptable and which further negatively impact on their self-esteem. They may feel unworthy and undeserving of a positive sexual relationship. The impact appears to be even more acute in female alcoholics for whom there is generally a greater stigma associated with alcoholism. Furthermore, many people (including the female alcoholic and male partner), may make some connection between female alcoholism and "sexual promiscuity".

Intimacy, communication and trust issues are very important, for both the recovering chemically dependent person and his/her partner. Such issues affect both the ability to function (e.g., potency, ability to orgasm), as well as those aspects of an adequate sexual relationship which are more than simply "equipment which functions".

Frequently, co-dependents have viewed sex as "awful" during the active dependence. If it is a wife, she has dealt with an alcoholic husband who has reeked of alcohol, who has ranged from less than a sensitive lover to brutal, and who may well have blamed his partner for all of his sexual problems. She (the partner), in turn, may now feel guilty because she is not feeling aroused and responsive to this "sick alcoholic who is currently sober and going to meetings". Frequently, the partner believes that when the alcoholic gets sober, there should be an immediate ability on her (partner's) part to be warm, intimate and caring, and a corresponding ability by the newly-recovering alcoholic to immediately be able to perform flawlessly.

If the ability to communicate and trust has disappeared during the active addiction, it will take some time to redevelop. Sometimes it was not present, even before the addiction, and therefore has to be established for the first time. The partner now is no longer able to place the responsibility for his own sexuality and any sexual dysfunction onto the actively using person . . . can no longer blame the alcoholic. People have to share with one another what they really feel, in spite of their fears.

Trust issues and their relationship to intimacy and sexuality are further complicated by fears that the alcoholic may relapse or that now that the alcoholic is sober, he/she will leave the partner for someone more desirable. Given the high rate of divorce among recovering alcoholic couples, this fear is not totally without foundation. Commonly, there is residual anger that the family member has felt during the active addiction which blocks current feelings of intimacy.

Frequently, communication problems exist because there has not been a feeling language employed between the chemically dependent person and his/her partner. These communication problems, the lack of trust, the residual anger, and a basic lack of interpersonal honesty which may have pre-dated or resulted from the dependence, become major obstacles to a satisfying relationship — sexual or otherwise. Looked at another way, the problems and the redevelopment of an adequate sexual relationship may be representative of the problems and the redevelopment of an overall relationship.

Unfortunately, in talking with many recovering chemically dependent people and partners who belong to A.A. and Al-Anon, the informal messages they have received about sex are: (1) "You don't talk about it" (2) "You don't get involved for a year" and (3) "It is equivalent to lust."

In the Book *Twelve Steps and Twelve Traditions*, when talking about Step 4, it is suggested that as a means of avoiding confusion, a list be made of the "Seven Deadly Sins," one of which is lust . . . what follows is a discussion about sex.

For those of us who have worked in the field and are aware of these admonitions which are provided to newly-recovering chemically dependent and significant others about sexuality, it is important that we reconsider them for accuracy, appropriateness and applicability. We are ethically bound to provide more appropriate suggestions.

"Don't get involved for one year!" What is magic about one year? Does the 365th day end at twelve midnight? If someone went to a residential program for treatment, is "one year" counted from the day of admission or the day of discharge? What is "involved"? A woman working in a halfway house confronted one of the residents who had recently visited a prostitute with the fact that he had breeched a house rule . . . that of not "getting involved". His response was that he was not involved, it was simply a "business proposition". Is he not correct?

Newly recovering alcoholics and significant others frequently have very strong needs for intimacy. How can these be met in a safe and appropriate fashion? Can we not experience intimacy which is not sexual? The very sharing and caring that occurs in A.A. and Al-Anon, and which makes them as effective as they are, speaks to intimacy.

One recommendation is to use a 4th Step inventory in part as a way of coming to know oneself sexually. In a regular inventory the individual gains knowledge which should aid them to not repeat the behaviors that caused them to feel guilt and anxiety. Should not the same thing be said for knowing yourself sexually? What is acceptable sexual behavior for one person may not be acceptable for another. It may, in fact, be a threat to sobriety. People are no more identical in their sexual values than in any other way.

Historically, A.A. was not only considerably more conservative, but the people who joined A.A. were a much more homogenous group than today. This homogeneity was found in age, socio-economic level, drinking and drug use patterns, source of referral, stage of illness, etc. At the very least, we are currently using some of the statements that may have been relevant 20 years ago on a population for which they are not nearly as meaningful today.

An analogy to sexuality issues and problems may be that of depression. Too frequently, alcoholics are diagnosed and treated as depressives because, in fact, they are depressed. In all probability, this depression is part of their disease of alcoholism. If the depression has not lifted after a period of recovery, then it must be re-evaluated because it may well be a separate affective disorder which does need attention. In a similar fashion, we can expect at least a disruption of sexual functioning, comfort levels, intimacy and communication during addiction and in early recovery. However, assuming that the people involved are in recovery programs and are making progress in other areas, such as self-image, communication, etc., there should be progress in the area of sexuality at about the same rate. If not, it is then time for a more formal assessment and possible referral for treatment.

"Going to more meetings" is not a solution to sexual problems. "Therapy" may be very threatening to many people in self-help groups. If the A.A. or Al-Anon member (although in my experience it would more likely be the A.A. member), believes that his "Program" is the answer to all of his problems, then going into therapy may be perceived as a betrayal of A.A., or the indication that A.A. is not working. Obviously this is not the case. If an alcoholic or significant other has an attack of appendicitis, going to more meetings is not going to help.

Just as recovering chemically dependent people and their families can arrive at a place of greater adjustment, emotional health and functioning than they ever did during or before the active dependence, there is no reason why this same thing cannot be true of their sexuality.

There are recovering people (both chemically dependent and co-dependent), who are obviously "turned on" with their lives and their recovery. There is no reason to believe that this same sort of enthusiasm is not possible and/or desirable relative to an individual's sexuality.

11

Family Factors and Warning Signs

BY

TERENCE T. GORSKI AND MERLENE MILLER

The family's involvement in the relapse syndrome is strongly influenced by co-alcoholism.

Co-alcoholism is a primary condition that results from the debilitating physiological stress produced by living in a committed relationship with an alcoholic or drug dependent person. The physiological stress is produced by the regular interaction of the family with the symptoms of alcoholism or drug dependence. It is important to remember that there are both alcohol and drug-induced symptoms, and withdrawal-induced symptoms. The alcoholic doesn't return to normal when he/she stops drinking. The long-term withdrawal, called Post Acute Withdrawal (PAW), can persist for six months to two years into sobriety. As a result, co-alcoholism can be aggravated by the symptoms of PAW.

The person suffering from co-alcoholism develops physical, psychological, behavioral and social symptoms as a result of attempting to adapt to and compensate for the debilitating effects of the physiological stress. As co-alcoholism progresses, the stress-related symptoms become habitual. The symptoms occur automatically and unconsciously. The symptoms also become self-reinforcing, that is, the presence of one co-alcoholic symptom will automatically trigger others. The co-alcoholism eventually becomes independent of the alcoholism or drug dependence that originally caused it. The symptoms of co-alcoholism will continue, even if the alcoholic becomes sober or if the co-alcoholic ends the relationship with the alcoholic.

The term "co-alcoholism" is sometimes used to refer only to the spouse of an alcoholic, and other terms such as "para-alcoholic" are being used to refer to children. In this article the term "co-alcoholic" is used to refer to *anyone whose life has become unmanageable as a result of living in a committed relationship with an alcoholic.*

Co-alcoholism is a definite and definable syndrome that is chronic and follows a predictable progression. When persons living in a committed relationship with an alcoholic attempt to control drinking and drinking behavior (over which they are powerless), they lose control over their own behavior (over which they can have the power) and their lives become unmanageable.

EARLY STAGE: Normal Problem-Solving and Attempts to Adjust to Heavy Drinking

Co-alcoholism results from the excessively high stress caused by living in a committed relationship with an alcoholic. Developing slowly at first, the co-alcoholic comes to accept the alcoholic's heavy drinking as normal. As problems develop, they attempt to use normal, culturally-defined problem-solving and coping mechanisms to deal with the symptoms of alcoholism. These symptoms of alcoholism do not respond to these methods. As a matter of fact, most normal family problem-solving and coping mechanisms will support or actually increase (enable) the level of alcoholism symptoms.

The normal reaction within any family to pain, to crisis and to the dysfunction of one member of the family is to reduce the pain, ease the crisis and to assist the dysfunctional member in order to protect the family. These responses do not make things better when the problem is alcoholism because these measures deprive the alcoholic of the painful learning experiences that bring an awareness that alcohol is creating problems in his or her life. At this stage, co-alcoholism is simply a reaction to the symptoms of the disease of alcoholism. It is a normal response to an abnormal situation.

MIDDLE STAGE: The Development of Habitual Self-Defeating Coping Mechanisms

When the culturally-prescribed responses to stress and crisis do not bring relief from the pain created by the alcoholism in the family, the concerned persons *try harder*. They do more of the same things; more often, more intensely, more desperately. They try to be more supportive, more helpful, more protective. They take on responsibilities of the alcoholic, not realizing that this enhances the alcoholic's tendency to become irresponsible.

The responses to drinking and drinking behavior become habitual, fixated and unconscious mechanisms for coping with the problem. They do the same things they have always done, even though those responses are not working. They adapt their own behavior and the functioning of the family to accommodate the drinking. But, things get worse instead of better, and the sense of failure intensifies the response. They experience frustration, anxiety and guilt. There is growing self-blame, self-concept degeneration and self-defeating behaviors. The co-alcoholic becomes isolated. Their focus is on drinking and drinking behavior and inadequate attempts to control these. They have little time to focus on anything else. The result is further removal from the world outside of their alcoholic family.

CHRONIC STAGE: Family Collapse and Stress Degenerations

The continued, habitual response to alcoholism in the family results in specific, repetitive, circular patterns of self-defeating behavior. These behavior patterns are independent and self-reinforcing, persisting even in the absence of continued alcoholism symptomatology.

The things the family members have done in a sincere effort to help have failed, and the resulting despair and guilt bring about confusion, chaos and the inability to interrupt dysfunctional behavior . . . even when they are aware that it is not helping. The thinking and behavior of the co-alcoholic is out of control, and these patterns will continue, even if the alcoholic gets sober, dies or is separated from the family.

Co-alcoholic degeneration is physical, psychological, behavioral, social and spiritual. The ineffective attempts to control drinking and drinking behavior elevate chronic stress to the point of producing stress-related physical illnesses, such as migraine headaches, ulcers and hypertension. This chronic stress may also result in nervous breakdown or other emotional or psychological illnesses. Out-of-control behavior manifests itself in an alcoholism-centered lifestyle that pervades all life activity, even that which seems unrelated to drinking or drinking behavior. *Social* degeneration occurs as the alcoholism focus interferes with relationships and social activity within and outside of the family. *Spiritual* degeneration results as the focus on the problem becomes so pervasive that there is no interest in anything beyond it, particularly concerns and needs related to a higher meaning of life.

Recovery from Co-alcoholism

Recovery from co-alcoholism means learning to accept and detach from the symptoms of alcoholism and learning to manage and control the symptoms of co-alcoholism. It means learning to focus on personal needs and personal growth, learning to respect and like oneself. It means learning to choose appropriate behavior. It means learning to be in control of one's life.

Because it is a chronic condition, co-alcoholism, like alcoholism, is subject to relapse. But conditions of co-alcoholic relapse may be more difficult to identify. Without an ongoing recovery program and proper care of oneself, old feelings and behaviors thought to be under control may surface and become out of control. Life again becomes unmanageable; the co-alcoholic is in relapse. The symptoms of the "co-alcoholic crisis" and the warning signs that precede it, are listed on the accompanying chart entitled *Relapse Warning Signs for Co-alcoholism.*

Co-alcoholism and Relapse

While each family member is responsible for his own recovery, the symptoms of alcoholism and co-alcoholism each impact upon the relapse potential of the other. Even if the alcoholic is no longer drinking and no longer experiencing the drinking-related symptoms of the disease, the post-acute withdrawal symptoms (PAW) affect, and are affected by, co-alcoholism. Both the symptoms of post-acute withdrawal and the symptoms of co-alcoholism are stress sensitive. Stress intensifies the symptoms and the symptoms intensify stress. As a result, the alcoholic and the co-alcoholic can become a stress-generating team that unknowingly and unconsciously complicate each other's recovery and create a high risk of relapse.

When a recovering co-alcoholic does not understand or recognize the symptoms of post-acute withdrawal being experienced by the recovering alcoholic, these symptoms can trigger a stress reaction that can lead to relapse for the entire family. The pattern is as follows:

1. The PAW symptoms of the alcoholic cause stress in the co-alcoholic.
2. The intensified stress in the co-alcoholic produces the early warning signs of a co-alcoholic crisis.
3. The co-alcoholic crisis triggers the early warning signs of relapse in the alcoholic.
4. The relapse warning signs produce even more stress for the co-alcoholic, and a full-blown co-alcoholic crisis ensues, marked by agitated, unpredictable and disruptive mood swings and behaviors.
5. The stress of living with a family member in active co-alcoholic crisis increases the stress levels of the alcoholic and causes the alcoholic relapse syndrome to get worse.
6. Both the alcoholic and the co-alcoholic eventually become incapacitated.

What can family members do to reduce the risk of their own relapse and the risk of relapse in the alcoholic?

1. Become informed about the disease of alcoholism, recovery and the symptoms that accompany recovery.
2. Recognize the symptoms of post-acute withdrawal as sobriety-based symptoms of alcoholism when they occur, rather than character defects, emotional disturbances or mental illness.
3. Accept and recognize the symptoms of co-alcoholism — your reaction to alcoholism in the family.
4. Become involved in Al-Anon and/or your own therapy, and develop a plan for your own recovery.
5. Learn to protect yourself from the stress that may be generated by the symptoms of post-acute withdrawal experienced by the recovering alcoholic.
6. Cooperate in plans to protect the recovering alcoholic from stress created by symptoms of co-alcoholism.
7. Be patient with your own recovery and the recovery of the alcoholic. None of you became ill overnight, and recovery will take place over a long period of time.
8. Recognize the relapse potential of alcoholism and co-alcoholism.
9. Develop a plan to prevent your own relapse and support relapse prevention plans for the alcoholic.

Relapse Warning Signs for Co-alcoholism

Early Warning Signs

Situational loss of daily structure.
Lack of personal care.
Inability to set and stick with limits with children.
Loss of constructive planning.
Indecision.
Compulsive behaviors.
Fatigue or lack of rest.

Return of unreasonable resentments.
Return of tendency to control people, situations, things.
Defensiveness.
Self-pity.
Over-spending.
Eating disorders — over or under.
Scapegoating.

Acute Co-alcoholic Crisis

Return of the fear and general anxiety.
Loss of belief in a "Higher Power".
Attendance at formal support meetings becomes sporadic.
Mind-racing.
Inability to construct a logical chain of thought.
Confusion.
Sleep disturbances.
Behavioral loss of control.
Uncontrollable mood swings.

Failure to maintain interpersonal (informal) support systems.
Feelings of loneliness, isolation.
Tunnel vision.
Return of periods of free-floating anxiety and/or panic attacks.
Health problems.
Use of medication or alcohol as a means to cope.
Total abandonment of support meetings, therapy sessions.

Debilitation

Inability to change behaviors in spite of conscious awareness that it is self-defeating.
Development of an "I don't care" attitude.

Complete loss of daily structure.
Despair and suicidal ideation.
Major physical collapse.
Major emotional collapse.

——12——

The Co-dependent Spouse

BY

J A N E T G E R I N G E R W O I T I T Z

*The following is excerpted from Dr. Woititz's book, **Marriage On The Rocks** (Health Communications, 1979).*

You cannot live with active alcoholism without being profoundly affected. Any human being who is bombarded with what you've been bombarded with is to be commended for sheer survival. You deserve a medal for the mere fact that you're around to tell the story. I know it has not been easy. You don't know from day to day — even from hour to hour — what to expect. You imagine all kinds of terrible things and, as often as not, you are right. You become obsessed with what will happen when he gets home (if he gets home). Your day is spent in emotional turmoil. Your head keeps spinning. You can't sleep. You don't eat properly. You look terrible. You withdraw from your friends. You snap at your children.

You're sick. You have developed a disease which we call co-alcoholism, which is every bit as damaging as alcoholism itself. Like alcoholism, it has its own symptoms. Anyone who has close contact with an alcoholic is affected by the disease, the degree being directly related to one's emotional nearness. Since you have the most continual and relevant contact with your husband, you are the most vulnerable.

As there are some patterns which described the alcoholic's behavior, there are also some patterns in your responses. No one close to an alcoholic escapes responding in at least some of the ways I will discuss. It is only a matter of degree. The following are the symptoms of co-alcoholism: denial, protectiveness, pity, concern about the drinker, embarrassment, avoiding drinking occasions, shift in relationship, guilt, obsession, continual worry, fear, lying, false hope, disappointment, euphoria, confusion, sex problems, anger, lethargy, hopelessness, self-pity, remorse and despair. As you read about these symptoms, try to identify the ones you have. Recognizing a problem is the first step in getting rid of it.

Denial

Denial is your biggest enemy. It seems impossible to believe that you are involved with an alcoholic. It simply cannot be true. If it cannot be true, it isn't true. You believe what you want to believe. You ignore reality. Because the alcoholic wants to face reality even less than you do, he helps you to be unrealistic. Denial is part of the disease for both you and your husband. He expends a great deal of energy denying the fact that he cannot control his drinking. He seems to control it for long periods of time. These periods grow shorter as the disease progresses, but he will convince both you and himself that he is the master of the bottle. Pure fantasy! The alcoholic does not seek help until he can no longer deny his lack of control and until the results of his behavior have been so horrifying he feels the pain despite the drug.

You don't look at the problem honestly either. You don't seek help until you are overwhelmed by the fear of violence, loss of income and uncertainty about what each day will bring. As the disease progresses, you take over more and more of the family responsibility. You try to maintain control over the situation and act as if everything is manageable. You deny the turmoil that exists within, as well as without, because denial is the most tolerable way to cope with an otherwise intolerable situation.

You go around in circles until the denial no longer works. You have no choice but to face facts when the weight of the evidence is overwhelming and the pain is too great to handle. Denial is part of the process that enables the disease to progress. This is true of any disease. How many unnecessary deaths have there been because people would not, for example, accept the fact that they had cancer? Disease flourishes in the virus of denial.

Denial makes life a lie. It distorts reality every bit as much for the non-alcoholic as the alcohol distorts reality for the alcoholic. If you choose to give up denial, you will experience an almost immediate sense of relief — get that monkey off your back. You can adjust to the truth. You don't have to like it, but you cannot deny it and be healthy.

Protectiveness, Concern About the Drinker

In the early stages of alcoholism, we are all very understanding. "Yes, dear, I know it's a jungle out there. Yes, you should have got the promotion. You work so hard with so little appreciation. Let me fix you a drink." You feel very sorry for your husband and his suffering. You worry about him and try to find solutions for his problems. There is no way to solve his problems, however, as he becomes more and more skillful at snatching defeat from the jaws of victory. If there is something to worry about or be angry about, he will find it. The injustice can be real or imagined. It doesn't matter.

Night after night, you get sucked in and lose sight of yourself in an attempt to pacify your alcoholic. After all, he *is* out there bringing home the paycheck and you owe it to him to make things as smooth for him at home as you possibly can. The fact that you've had a rough day too is not important. It is part of your role to make the world right for your husband. Your needs are not important.

Jean B. remembers: "That's what my husband told me. You know what else? I believed him. And more and more I became less and less. I became a servant in my own home. I had no needs. But I

sure had a good case of colitis. Those feelings that I denied I had
were eating my guts out. I was so concerned for my husband that
I would bleed. Everything was being drained out of me. We non-
persons do things like that. But not anymore!"

Embarrassment, Avoiding Drinking Occasions

What other people think of us seems to be very important — far
more important, in fact, than what we think of ourselves. We
assume that others are judging us by our own behavior and by the
behavior of those around us, especially that of our family. When I
bragged about my youngest son walking at nine months, was I
saying, "He's terrific," or was I saying, "I'm terrific"? By the same
token, when the older kids run into trouble at school, unless I
make a conscious effort to separate myself from them, I consider it
a negative reflection on me as a parent. Since you are probably like
most people, when your alcoholic husband behaves outrageously,
you're embarrassed. You make excuses and wish you were
invisible. You don't feel that you can go home, leaving the "life of
the party" behind. A number of these experiences will cause you to
feel insecure and afraid of social situations where there is drinking.
Eventually, you want to avoid such situations altogether. The
embarrassment is too great. You are, in effect, taking responsibility
for his behavior. The truth is that you can really only take
responsibility for your own behavior. At this point, that statement
doesn't make much sense. You also don't understand that other
people often don't know that your husband's behavior humiliates
you. Other people's drunken husbands don't bother me. Sometimes I enjoy them because I don't have to go home with them.

You also can't enjoy the party because you're watching him all
the time, suggesting that maybe he's had enough, trying to get him
to leave, insisting on driving. It reaches a point where it's just not
worth going in the first place. If you can't have a good time, why
bother? Consequently, you feel sorry for yourself and nurse your
wounds.

Shift in Relationship — Domination, Take-over,
Self-absorptive Activities

As the disease progresses, the alcoholic assumes less and less
responsibility. The relationship between you and your husband

and you and your children changes. You take over more and more. You try to become both mother and father to your children. This is not possible. A mother simply cannot be a father. She is just not built for it. A mother can only be the best mother she is able to be. When she tries to be a father too, she takes on an impossible task. Not only is it unrealistic, it is destructive to the children. She causes confusion in their minds and wears herself out.

You become more and more in charge, and make virtually all the decisions in the house. The alcoholic eventually becomes yet another child. And although you dominate him as you would a child, you become angry and resentful when he does not behave like an adult.

After taking over, it is not unusual for you to get invovled in lots of activities outside the home. You are continually busy. These self-absorptive activities are a form of escape. Even if what you are doing is very productive, your motive is less to be helpful than to avoid thinking.

Guilt

The alcoholic is expert at projecting his own guilt feelings onto you. You become expert at accepting them. When he avoids responsibility for his behavior, yelling, "You drive me to drink!" you take it on yourself.

When you hear how terrible you are over a period of time, it is almost impossible not to believe it. As a result, much of what the alcoholic says is internalized and you become ridden with guilt. The alcoholic knows just where you are vulnerable and pushes those buttons.

Obsession, Continual Worry

As the disease occupies more and more of the alcoholic's thoughts, it has the same effect on you. Life is no longer predictable and you are continually worried. What will happen next? Will he be caught drinking on the job? Will he be fired? Where is he? Will he be home on time? Will he get hurt? Where will he go? Will he be violent? How can I get him to stop drinking? Where have I gone wrong? Is there another woman? Should I leave him? Why do I love him? Is there a way out?

You go through the motion of living, but your mind is elsewhere — always on the alcoholic. This obsession is a waste of energy, because it solves nothing. It only makes the whole family sicker, more involved in the emotional orbit of your husband.

Fear

Anxiety and fear are usually present in the alcoholic home. Some of these fears are groundless, and some are well-founded, such as: Can I make it alone? Will he beat me? What if he loses his job?

I know a woman whose husband chained the doors when she left the house so she couldn't get back in. At first, she was afraid to leave because the thought of being locked out with her children locked in terrified her. Later on, she learned to carry a screwdriver and undo the latch. Her fear, once confronted, was manageable.

Many women lose confidence in themselves as a result of living with an alcoholic. Then they become fearful and anxious. Situations that at one time were not at all threatening become overwhelming. These women become more and more the victims of their nameless fears. I know some women living with active alcoholics who are terrified of being alone, others who are afraid to leave the house. They can't explain why, but the fear overwhelms them. It's terrible to live in fear. It renders us immobile. It makes us behave in irrational ways. One act out of fear leads to another, and we lose control of our lives. We start spinning our wheels with no place to go.

Lying

Lying is a way of life in an alcoholic home. You lie in order to protect the alcoholic. You tell his boss, "I'm sorry, he won't be in to work today. He has the flu." You explain to your neighbor, "I don't know how the lamp got broken. The cat must have knocked it over."

The most destructive of all are the lies that are not really lies. They are truthful in intent but not in execution. The alcoholic says, "I will be home at 6:00 for dinner!" He is not lying. He fully intends to be home at 6:00 for dinner. But he does not arrive home at 6:00, because there is a world of difference between his intent and his ability to carry it out.

This kind of behavior adds greatly to the confusion and disorganization of your family. Truth loses its meaning, and perceptions of reality become distorted. You simply do not know what to believe. In the end, you believe pretty much what you want to believe. This leads to continually setting yourself up for a letdown. He is so convincing, and you would rather believe him than the evidence of last week's burnt dinner or unused theater tickets. That can all change, however. You can learn to eat and go to the theater alone if you have to. But you have to get well first.

False Hope, Disappointment, Euphoria

Part of what throws the alcoholic's family into confusion and despair is the building up of hopes and the subsequent disappointment. The family, unable to accept reality, lives in fantasy. You think of your alcoholic husband in terms of what he was or could be. When he makes a promise you respond as if he were that person. When he does not fulfill his promise, you are let down much more than you would be if you had not believed him in the first place. If he does keep his promise, you are so excited you become euphoric. This, of course, sets you up for greater disappointment the next time. The alternating feelings of false hope, disappointment and euphoria add to your confusion and fear.

You really believed that *this* time he would follow through. You were getting along so well. He hadn't had a drink in two weeks. *This time it would be different.* How many times have you said those words to yourself? How many times has the alcoholic said those words to himself? Yes, it's different. It's worse. The disease progresses. You are not in control. Your husband is not really in control. The alcohol is in control — if you allow it to be.

Confusion

You become confused when you live with an alcoholic. You don't know what to believe or what to expect. Since he is pulling the strings, you are dancing to a very inconsistent tune. Your sense of what is real becomes distorted. Everyday is more unmanageable, a living nightmare.

It is very hard for you to think straight. In fact, it is very hard for you to think at all. You can't turn your head off, yet you can't come up with any answers. You're on a treadmill; but you don't know where you got on, and you don't know how to get off. You start to wonder where it is all going to end. "Am I losing my mind?" you ask yourself. "Maybe I am going crazy. No sane person would live this way." And you just may be right.

Sex Problems

As communication in other areas of your marriage breaks down, the physical expression of closeness breaks down as well. You use sex as a weapon. You withhold sex if your husband doesn't behave himself. He can't have you in bed if he's going to drink like that. "Go to bed with your mistress or the bottle!" you think.

You may be repulsed by the smell of the liquor, which is reason enough to reject his overtures. You assume he wants you out of lust and not love anyway. You may, however, submit to him because you figure that if he is sexually satisfied, he will go to sleep and leave you alone. You may also think in terms of your wifely role and responsibility. So you have the choice of feeling guilty or degraded. Once again, your self-esteem has been reduced.

Sexual abuse is not uncommon. Women submit to behavior they would resist if they had any self-respect left. Clients tell me of actions resulting in the need for medical attention. It is hard for them even to tell me what happened. But these unfortunate women gather their courage to tell me so that I can give them permission not to allow it to happen again. I give my client permission to be a person.

It is not unusual for the alcoholic to have an affair. He complains, "My wife doesn't understand me." You sure as hell don't! "She doesn't want me in bed." Well, he's right. "She won't drink with me." You tried it, but you've developed an aversion to the stuff by this time. It doesn't matter that the affair is a symptom of the disease — you are shattered. Your identity is so tied up with him that you are beside yourself. "I'm obviously not much of a woman," you conclude. "If I were, this affair would not have happened." Your self-image thus takes another downward plunge. You're a bad wife, mother, housekeeper and now — you've lost your sexuality. You're a nothing. Baloney! You're a victim. You're a casualty of co-alcoholism.

Some couples are able to maintain a satisfying sex life until the later stages of the disease, when the husband becomes impotent. The problem here is that you think that because you can be so loving in bed, everything else will be all right. This hope, too, is shattered. Your expectations get you into trouble and you can only be disappointed. There can be no winning until you learn how to give up your false hopes and live in the moment. You will.

Anger

Anger, in one form or another, is always present in the alcoholic home. The tension is thick enough to cut with a knife. What will he say? What will he do? I'll kill him if he doesn't leave me alone. Will he damage the car? Will he wake up the kids? Should I ask him for the money? All these uncertainties lead to anger with people you are not really angry at. You become rigid and distrustful. Rage consumes you without a satisfying outlet. Anyone who walks into your house can feel the angry vibrations. There is no escape from it. Who ever thought you would turn into such a self-righteous witch?

This tension, however, does not always show itself in your behavior. If you are living with violence, you may keep it inside rather than risk an assault. It's a difficult but realistic choice. If it is inner directed, that is, if you continually keep your mouth shut even though you feel the need to explode, the tension will probably make you physically ill. Colitis, gastritis and ulcers are not uncommon in families of alcoholics.

Lethargy, Hopelessness, Self-pity, Remorse, Despair

No matter what you do, no matter how hard you try, it isn't enough. You give and you give as if the well has no bottom. After a while, you give up. What's the difference? Nothing you do will change anything. You are physically and mentally exhausted. You are tired of carrying the world on your shoulders. You just can't do it anymore. You reach a point where you lose interest in everything.

Your emotional energy is drained, and you feel hopeless and alone. You are filled with self-pity and remorse. Getting through each day becomes a chore. Getting out of bed and getting dressed are overwhelming tasks. What's the use of going on? It simply isn't worth it, you think. Consequently, you give up. You withdraw into an isolated existence.

When you reach this point of despair, you yourself may start drinking or taking drugs. It's incredible, but the alcohol wins again. You don't care anymore, and you feel as if you can't face another day. Your problems are too great. Your life has become totally unmanageable. You want out.

Identify with any of this? Any of it have any special meaning to you? You betcha! I give you my word, I haven't been in your house. But I've been in a hundred other houses, and I've talked to a hundred other women who have lived your life. You're not alone. It's a big and not very exclusive club.

I am reminded of the airline pilot who said to his passengers, "I have some good news and I have some bad news. The bad news is . . . we're lost. The good news is . . . we're making excellent time." It's amazing how much you expend going round and round in circles. You may not believe it now, but you have the power to say, "Hey, wait a minute. I want to get off."